WHEN THIS

An anthology in aid of the Rennie Grove
Hospice Care

Edited by Jan Moran Neil
&
Adrian Spalding

Creative Ink Publishing

First Edition: *WHEN THIS IS ALL OVER …*
First published in Great Britain in 2021 by:
Creative Ink Publishing
www.janmoranneil.co.uk
www.adrianspalding.co.uk

British Library Cataloguing in Publication Data. A CIP record
for this book can be obtained from the British Library.

Cover photo: by kind permission of Linda Ralph.

For all those who had to go out to work.
And for all the thousands of lost souls.
For the readers of the future and for the writers herein.

Acknowledgements:

For disseminating the details of this anthology:

Tina Jackson: Assistant Editor of *Writing Magazine*
Jill Wallis: last Editor of *Rhyme & Reason* magazine
Hazel Bendon: Senior Community Fundraiser at the *Rennie Grove Hospice Care*
Kirsty Jackson: *Cranthorpe Millner Publishers*
Karen Gray-Kilfoil: *Scribblers,* Cape Town, South Africa
Michelle Gunner: *Metroland Poets*

For Proof Reading: Jane MacKinnon
For Marketing: Suzie Cullen
For Cover Photo: Linda Ralph
For Amazon Kindle account: Head Office at the *Rennie Grove Hospice Care*
Thank you.

Any donations to:
Account Name – The Iain Rennie Hospice at Home Appeal;
Sort code – 20-02-06; Account No – 10511374

All services have been given free of charge. All printing costs covered by Creative Ink Publishing. All takings after Amazon go to the charity.

If you enjoy this anthology then please leave a review on Amazon and spread the word to increase sales.

Table of Contents

Editorial
To the Reader a Hundred Years Hence
and to the Reader Now

It was during one of those first lockdown walks when we were dodging joggers and cyclists that the idea of this anthology came to me: a historical document; a Covid-19 time capsule. It's intended to be recollections of a year when our global civil liberties were curtailed; when often we didn't have access to regular medical care, education or public worship; when we were unable to travel, touch, sing or celebrate with one another; unable to fully grieve for those we lost and when many lived, by and large, in fear. That's a long sentence and so it has been. And we didn't see it coming.

The parent of this anthology is the once annual *Rhyme & Reason* which during its lifetime of 27 years raised over £60,000 for formerly the Iain Rennie Hospice at Home and now the Rennie Grove Hospice Care. Having been a founder editor of that little gem, the idea of a charity Covid-19 anthology was spawned in my mind. People could park their feelings about the pandemic. We could raise money through spreading our words, and not the virus, for nurses who came into the home. Home is where we had to stay and paradoxically was the very place that Covid-19 spread so plentifully. And yet the nurses have kept on nursing.

And writers keep on writing. This book includes words from: a BAFTA award-winning screenwriter; a founder member of *Poets on the Underground* and *Signal Award* winner; a *Forward* shortlisted poet; a renowned children's TV writer; many published poets and authors as well as doctors and nurses and frontline workers. My co-editor Adrian Spalding and I thank them all for their generosity of spirit. But it is the writers who do not consider themselves writers to whom we particularly wish to doff our 2020-2021 hats. People who had the courage to let their words sit alongside other people who have writing certificates; people from New Zealand to Newcastle who have maybe not taken pen to paper or placed hands on laptops to tell their stories since they were at school. And indeed some of the writers are still at school and hoping the schools will remain open. Rainbow writers all.

Moving from first lockdown in March 2020 to the lifting of restrictions in the spring of 2021 we had 421 submissions from across the world and across the year. It was therefore appropriate to split the book into the four seasons.

Spring: when lockdown was born, home schooling hit us and a new vocabulary was invented. When we began to appreciate a clearer air and respect for nature.

Summer: 'Eat Out to Help Out' but learnt new recipes, missed weddings, missed libraries, missed theatre and sport; spent lots of time in the garden, the loft, cleaning out cupboards and missing things.

Autumn: missed travel and wished to be as free as the birds; missed our loved ones and came to terms with Perspex. But there's a clear message of gratitude for those who had to go out to work and that we are still standing.

Winter: This editor did not want to slice away at any of those sharp-edged feelings. She just crossed the 'i's' and dotted the 't's'. Then came the vaccine and hope … We still do. And the colour of hope is yellow.

My co-editor Adrian Spalding www.adrianspalding.co.uk has safely guided this book into your hands and helped make an idea a reality. I have known Adrian since I was six. We were in the same class at primary school. Together, using techniques we could have only dreamt about as children, we have created this book. You in the future will regard today's cutting-edge technology as primitive. We, here, can only imagine what you will achieve. We send our words through time and space so you might understand our world.

So where to begin? Well, as Glinda the Good Witch in L Frank Baum's *The Wizard of Oz* said, 'It's always best to begin at the beginning …' When was that? The day before the first UK lockdown was born: Mother's Day 2020.

Here we go …

Warmest wishes across the years,
Jan Moran Neil MSt Cantab www.janmoranneil.co.uk

Author, playwright, editor, tutor, publisher and sometime actress. Jan's novel 'Shakespeare's Clock'/Cranthorpe Millner will be available on Amazon and from all major bookstores this autumn 2021.

SPRING

'DAFFODILS
THAT COME BEFORE THE SWALLOW DARES
AND TAKE THE WINDS OF MARCH WITH BEAUTY'

SHAKESPEARE'S 'THE WINTER'S TALE'

Born in the Time of Coronavirus by Jan Moran Neil

Welcome to this extraordinary globe,
Eleanor Rose.
And always remember, Ellie
there is a pharmacy inside your wonderful body.

For Mother by Ashley May

Take me to the native land,
where I can sit on a golden throne made of family and love.
Where the sunshine is gold and the moon weeps
on to the waves caressing the world with gentle, soft tickles
of the night.
Let me scream and shout with pride for my family and my
land, we will never die.
I love you, Mother. Don't ever forget the endless arguments,
the endless love that keeps us safe.
Let's take a ride to the ocean and sing along to your favourite
song.
I love Mother forever and ever,
the never ending story of love
and gold eyes that have wept,
but smile upon the grey skies.

- Happy Mother's Day. I love you.
- Ashley, your son forever. 22nd March 2020

Ashley is from East Sussex and wrote this poem for his mother whilst he was in hospital with Covid-19.

Mothers Meeting by Esther May Greenberg

More than ever my mother has been on mind during this pandemic. Having lost my mother nineteen years ago today, when I was only seventeen, I thought I had prepared myself emotionally for being without her at the most significant times in my life. But when I sat in a cold, dark, 90s' looking nursing room filled with pine cupboards, slightly sticky floors and the smell of disinfectant lingering in the air, I seemed to sense my mother's presence most acutely. This was my first face-to-face midwife appointment. Unfortunately I had to be alone due to the current situation. She asked me why I was carrying such a large bag. I told her, 'Because this is my first appointment and I am carrying a large photo of my mother in my bag as she is no longer with us'.

The midwife smiled with her eyes – as this was all I could see as she held test tubes of blood she had taken from me – and she said, 'My love. She is in here'.

It wasn't until I was driving home that I realized she was saying that my mother was in my blood and not in the test tubes she was waving in front of me. It was then that I realized what it meant to be a mother.

Written on 5th February 2021. Patricia Mary Arnold Greenberg (27th August 1951- 5th February 2002)

Esther has been in several Creative Ink plays: 'Blackberry Promises', 'Brave Hearts & Baggage', 'The Deadly Factor' and 'Dear John, Dear Anyone…' film. She has appeared in the film 'The Imitation Game'. She enjoys: teaching drama, photography and voice over work. She is expecting her first baby in August 2021.

Birth Day by Chrissie Thomas

As I held my newborn grandchild a new hope sprang up. I gazed in wonder at this new life, so precious, so perfect; I could see my own child, thirty some odd years ago in a different world. And I held this baby's tiny hand and spoke to him of new life, new times ahead when we would once more sit on verdant grass in fragrant meadows, by flowing streams and celebrate a birthday, an anniversary and he would learn how perfect life can be.

The nurses ask me, will they remember us after all this? Or will they become complacent once more, take us for granted, take life for granted?

'Personally,' I said, 'I will live in hope'.

Chrissie has been a teacher for most of her life, working in an assortment of schools and educational establishments. Currently she works as a private tutor, teaching GCSE and A-level. She lives in Grantham, Lincolnshire.

Twenty Seconds Haiku by Moyra Zaman

Drains clogged with *'Happy Birthdays'*; hands cleansed and clapping in isolation.

For Mum by Eddie Molloy

We used to have a routine day to day.
Now I watch you whilst you fade away.
You no longer understand we can't do the things we used to do.
No coffee dates with friends. No dinner dates just me and you.
Your routine is no more. Now when I leave you in the house
I have to double lock the door. So when I see you slumped in that chair
it breaks my heart to see that vacant stare.

No one really knows what you're going through.
I feel so helpless because I can't help you.
When you stand there with a tea bag in your hand not knowing why
I have to bite my lip as it makes me want to cry.
You repeat yourself until I can't take it anymore.
I turn around and stop you putting cat food on the floor.
I try not to shout and tell you 'It doesn't go there'.
You stand and look at me with that vacant stare.

When the mum I knew I thought was dead and gone
you give me that look that just proves me wrong.
Then I have you back for five minutes exact.
Although it doesn't take long before again you're gone.
I ask you a simple question. You reply 'I don't know and I don't care'.
Followed by that vacant stare.

As the lockdown ends and people get back to the things they
used to do
I don't think that will be the case for me and for you.
I know you feel the same too. I can see it inside of you:
somewhere deep inside there. It's between that vacant stare.

*Nina Molloy was diagnosed with Alzheimers in 2015. Eddie is
one of his mum's full-time carers. He raised £2000 for the
Alzheimer's Society running in the Birmingham Half Marathon.
He writes that he has performed in three productions with the
Creative Ink family.*

Burst of Life by Mary Fletcher

It's almost time. Mum twitches back the curtain, scours the street for signs of life then tightens her dressing gown woollen armour. 'I'm not doing it if no one else is.'

Dad grumbles on the sofa, calls it daft. I threaten to go it alone, become a source of neighbourly gossip. They've not moved. Minutes pass. I head for the upstairs window. Badger my parents until they do the same. We stumble up, a procession of awkward, shy support. 7.58pm.

Pale faces peer out from behind distant doorways as feet toe sterile boundaries. 'Open the window!' I say.

Dad wrestles with the sticky lock as another minute passes. He springs it open to brittle clapping. It's faint, almost an apology, but it's enough. Another set of hands joins in then another. The sound builds, palms and hopes colliding until the air swells with noise. People cheer. Thunderous applause and laughter cross social distances. I holler. Even as my skin burns, I don't want to stop.

It's a burst of life within the stasis. It's the belief that everything will be all right. As we stand and shout and clap, it's the knowledge that we'll get through this because, 'Thank you, NHS'.

Mary is an emerging writer based in Stoke-on-Trent, Staffordshire. When she is not writing short stories and novels, she can be found drinking tea or updating her blog.
www.medium.com@MaryLouWrites.

Birthday Wish by Sarah Barthélémy

Today's my birthday. I sit on the edge of the land near Calais, where the Channel meets the North Sea, and stare at the water. It's deceptively blue today. Black seal heads bob here and there, and the cliffs of Dover rise clearly like golden columns in the sunshine.

How I long to be there, on the other side. I imagine covering myself with goose fat and swimming across. Some do. But it's the most dangerous strait in the world. And I actually can't swim very far at all. So, I sit and gaze and try not to let this unexpected barrier break my heart. Never did I think the day would come that I wouldn't be allowed into my own country.

Afterwards, we drive back home. We pass three migrants walking along the motorway, heading to Calais. They, too, will see how close the cliffs of Dover are. Then I remember about a young man, who died the other day, rowing across the Channel in an inflatable dinghy with spades for oars. He had had no other hope left. How small my own temporary heartbreak suddenly seems.

Sarah is a British-born translator, also working on her first middle grade novel. She lives in St Omer, near Calais.

Happy Birthday, Diya by Fazlyn Fester

I wrote to my only grandchild, Diya, for her fifth birthday on Monday 1st June 2020. A few days earlier, in a family Zoom meeting, she asked that I teach her to knit. I remember that it was the first day of level three lockdown restrictions (in South Africa) and I was watching the news focus on queues outside liquor stores. People had been waiting for the liquor stores to open from as early as six am. Since 27th March, the start of National Lockdown, all sales of liquor had been banned in South Africa.

Dearest Diya, I can't believe you are five years old! I would like nothing more than to hold you and hug you and say 'Happy Birthday' in person. But the coronavirus has changed all that. Maybe one day soon this bad coronavirus will go away, or better still, we will have a vaccine to combat it and everyone will be safe. Until then we must wear a face mask when outside in public, wash our hands a lot and keep two metres away from people.

My dream has always been to teach you to play the ukulele and to enjoy music. You have always had rhythm and used to sway to music from the age of six months already. Now I wish I could teach you to knit, but because of the coronavirus, we cannot be together. So, for your birthday I have sent you knitting needles, wool and a DVD which you can watch. Watch it as many times as you like. Maybe you can start knitting something easy, like a scarf for your favourite doll. Soon we will get together and be a family again. Until then – big hugs and have a wonderful birthday!

Lots of love, Ma.

Fazlyn is a retired nurse and has been to Scribblers' meetings in Fish Hoek, Cape Town, South Africa.

For Aurora and Ophelia by Maureen Bradley

I will gaze deeply into your eyes.
You may both look back in surprise.
My arms will hold you far too tight
and squeeze you as hard as I might.
In my heart is where you have both been
until now not allowed to be seen.
To not be with you was hard to bear
so forgive me if I just take a while and stare.
Patience paid off and the lucky ones are we:
I can now be with you and you can now be with me.

Maureen is from Kingswinford, West Midlands and after meeting Jan when she was lecturing on cruise ships travelled weekly to Creative Ink classes. Maureen has twin granddaughters born a month before lockdown and shining lights in these dark times.

Just a Suggestion by A'O'E'

I want to give you a birthday treat.
Come up to town. Where shall we meet?
At the Aldwych, Big Ben, Covent Garden at ten?
Downing Street or the Docks?
(But not in our bestest of frocks!)
Do you fancy Earls Court or Fleet Street?
The Guild Hall or Greek Street?
Horse Guards Parade?
Leicester Square, Marble Arch?
(Have a drink in a bar if we get parched?)
Olympia, Oxford Street?
Perhaps tea with the Queen?
The V&A I have never seen.
You make the choice: just you and me.
Where shall it be?

I think I'd rather go to Folkestone.
Anywhere but home.

A'O'E trained at the Mathay School of Music in Liverpool. She lives in Beaconsfield, Buckinghamshire and has been writing voraciously for donkey's years. Her humorous poetry has been performed by 'Rhyme & Reason'.

Birthday Cake by Jan Moran Neil

I can see you and hear you
but I can't smell you or feel you.
I know you are not coming today
but I will bake you a cake
and post it the old-fashioned way.
Then we can toast the caramel salted years
and in tandem taste the hard work
our tongues have done.

Twenty Seconds Haiku by Moyra Zaman

'Happy Birthday' to me
counts the hand-washing minutes,
aging me quickly.

The Fuss About Birthdays by Tom Johnson

If and when we have managed to defeat Covid-19 or, more likely, have learned to live with it, we will have a whole year to catch up with. Friends we haven't been able to meet; family we can only see at a distance and grandchildren we have forgotten how to hug.

We have developed skills with Zoom, WhatsApp, Instagram and other social media. We have telephoned old friends to check on their well-being and have contributed to the local foodbank in support of the needy. Sadly, we have also missed special celebrations, weddings, important birthdays and sometimes funerals which have left many feeling bereft and disappointed; special birthdays planned well in advance for family and friends now postponed or cancelled. One such 80th birthday prompted the following reflection:

Why all the fuss about birthdays?
Does it matter how old we are?
I'd rather be celebrating friendship
with our families both near and afar.
OK, this one ends with a zero
instead of a nine or an eight
but surely it matters very little
if I cannot spend time with a mate.
I am truly grateful for friendship,
for folk I have known a long time
and I thank you all for remembering me
as I slip into steady decline.
If this sounds a little bit maudlin
and lacking any trace of cheer

then please forgive me as a poet,
and if you're offering, I'll have a beer.

So perhaps we should now start to look forward, remembering newly-found friends and acquaintances; new coping methods and gratitude when things go right. It's the younger generations that will bear the brunt of this awful time but perhaps they will show us oldies how to cope with adversity. They will need our wisdom and encouragement and we will need their positive outlook.

God bless you all.

Tom was born in Hertfordshire and has lived in Beaconsfield, Buckinghamshire for 42 years. He has been involved with Rennie Grove – formerly the Iain Rennie Hospice – for over 30 years as Trustee, Vice Chair, Chairman of Fundraising Strategy and Treasurer of Beaconsfield Fundraising Group. He writes: 'When I had a proper job I was MD of an engineering service company in the aerospace industry'.

Our Next Breath by Jim Dening

From knowledge or memory
or from ancient instinct
we perform at each instant
the action necessary, not because
we are free and conscious
in that moment,
but swept onward
within the assembly of matter
we call the universe.
There is no moment:
past and future join up
in a moving surface – and we?
We ride on the wave
of our next breath.

Jim grew up near Chester and now lives in Ledbury in the west of England. He has lived in Paris and in southern France and also writes in French. For many years he lived near Amersham, Bucks, and created a publishing business concerned with tracing the records of international boundaries and the disputes that arose over territories arbitrarily divided. Publications: 'The accident of birth', 'pebbles, debris' (2003); 'Dealing with the edge'; (2011); 'Les chemins d'ici'/'The roads round here' (2016) (bilingual in French and English).

Beginnings by Marion Caragounis

I believe in beginnings. For me the fat lady never sings because the curtains always remain open for the next act to proceed. I can see that the pattern of my life is one of endings and beginnings accompanied by emotions that are as varied as the events that initiated them.

Here are a few of my beginnings, all precipitated by some kind of an ending: marriage, living alone again, moving home ten times, new friends, new marriage and eventually moving to Greece resulting in more unexpected beginnings. Shakespeare described seven stages of life in *As You Like It*. But I didn't like his description of life as a series of short performances slowly deteriorating into oblivion.

As an octogenarian I avoid reading obituaries. They suggest that I am on 'borrowed time'. Another moot point. I believe I am in 'appointed time' and still 'on stage' about to move on to the next act – to use his metaphor.

Of course eventually life as I know it will be over, but as a Christian I will be expecting another new beginning to follow, unlike anything that has gone before. It will be my voice singing that closing song because I believe in beginnings.

Marion has retired to Greece where she writes articles, poetry and hymns mostly for pleasure. She has published her poetry collection 'Shafts of Son Light'.

The Selfish Isolator by Simon Tindale

Week One

I bought all the bog roll in town.
There's not quite enough to go round.
Perhaps I should issue
you all with one tissue
to use when the shit's going down.

Week Two

They cancelled my spring holiday.
The football's postponed until May.
The pubs are all shut.
I've a pain in my butt
but the doctor says, 'Please stay away'.

Week Three

Someone is murdering the Bangles.
Now Angels is going through the mangle.
'Stayin' Alive'
follows 'I Will Survive'.
I'd rather hear Cats being strangled.

Week Four

The neighbour's no good at home schooling.
It's only himself that he's fooling.
Those ignorant brats
won't learn English or Maths;
his bad language needs overruling.

Week Five

Our leaders are out of their depth.
Their vision lacks clarity and breadth.
Is it worth jumping in
when you're struggling to swim?
Are you better off saving your breath?

Week Six

You may be surprised that this loner
signed up to become a blood donor.
A gallon of ale's
been instilled in these veins.
I do hope it chokes the corona.

    Simon was born in Sunderland, North East England, wrote songs in south London, found poetry in West Yorkshire and initially read this poem last summer at the Ledbury Festival 'Lockdown Lit' event.

Baggy Point by Laurence Cooper

The tyres crunch the gravel of your final stop,
beyond the flotsam of ice cream and surf shops
in Croyde. The road runs out, into this car park
at the start of the Point, just short of Morte Bay.
The sky ahead is deathly dark,

burdened with rain. A whale bone marks the way
from where you have to abandon your car and pay.
You wonder if it will all be a lamentable waste
of time; of energy. The shark has your foot again.
The cold bites your face.

This headland is not here for your diversion.
It directs you to walk in pilgrim contemplation.
There are no otters. Lundy Island cannot be seen.
Provocative gusts lash the gorse with sea foam,
spray, moans and screams

as all winds meet here. All emotions understood
and held. Shout joy or agony at the billows and flood.
All your dead ends delivered you to this wild energy.
Your emptiness consummated by a raw delight
and complete, yet alien, empathy.

How could it be otherwise than this? Your flesh
troubled and challenged but your heart is refreshed.
Surrender your plans, what you are doing tonight.
Lean your whole being in the wind's rough hand
and the breath of life.

Written just before lockdown March 2020.

Laurence is based in Birmingham but is moving south this year, transferring to the Bar after a career in commercial and charity work. When this is all over, he hopes to be undertaking pupillage at 3 Dr Johnson's Buildings, Temple. Laurence writes for 'Counsel' magazine and other legal publications, and is a member of Coventry Live Poets.

The World Has Had Enough by Vanessa Moon

The world had had enough. 'Stop,' she said as her invisible warriors silently went to work. 'That's enough.'

The sea and the air agreed with her. The birds took on the role of sentinel, viewing the place from above, as the people retreated to their houses and remembered how to be kind, and life became simple. People shared food and clothes with the homeless man as he walked in socks, pulling his life possessions behind him, damp after the rain.

'Wait,' said the earth as the people grew impatient. 'There is magic happening. It is not time.'

So the people became still and a calm passed over the land, touching everyone gently. The people who had become spoilt rebelled and struggled in the slow time, but gradually, like a flower unfurling, they too dropped heavy into their bodies and left the flying for the birds. The sea noisily reminded people of her presence as the waves pounded on the empty beach.

'Enough,' she said, joining in with the wind. 'Enough,' she said and the water sparkled and the fish swam and the dolphins played in the deep water as it rained and rained because the sun too had had enough, leaving us alone with ourselves to think about all we had done and not done.

So time stretched out before us, and we settled into it and started noticing the tiny things, things of great beauty around us all the time which so many had stopped seeing in their rush to be somewhere else. And the flowers said thank you to the rain, their fat spring heads bobbing gently in the wind as we waited for the sun to shine.

Vanessa is a retired psychotherapist and a painter and furniture restorer in a former life. Her kids are grown up so she is free to concentrate on writing, both academic and creative.

What Is Happening by Anthony Saunders

For me the fear of the pandemic and lockdown started at the end of February 2020. People were going crazy and panic buying, which then resulted in shops putting limits on how many items people could buy and seeing empty shelves. Then I started seeing people wearing masks. Some of them did look cool but it was kind of scary and it did freak me out. It frightened me. March came and things started changing and change really stresses me out as I am autistic. I find it hard having to have temperatures checked before entering my clubs and we had to start to use hand sanitizer more. I was then told I could not see my fiancée for a while. When it came to going home that day I was very sad … neither of us wanted me to go home. It was also the last time I went on the bus to my home. My clubs I go to stopped. I stopped seeing my friends. My friends are really important to me. Then it happened … lockdown. I got so confused and upset.

My friends messaged me to check how I was and explain more. I found the first couple of weeks really hard as my routine had suddenly changed. What really helped was playing Mario Kart online with my friends. Whenever I heard that Boris was going to do an announcement I got scared about what he would say and I would end up confused and stressed about it. But one of my best friends would message me with an easier explanation which helped a lot.

Anthony is 30 years old, autistic, friend to everyone.

Play No Ball by Gerard Benson

What a wall!
Play No Ball.
It tells us all.
Play No Ball.
By Order!

Lick no lolly.
Skip no rope.
Nurse no dolly.
Wish no hope.
Hop no scotch.
Ring no bell.
Telly no watch.
Joke no tell.
Fight no friend.
Up no make.
Penny no lend.
Hand no shake.
Tyre no pump.
Down no fall.
Up no jump.
Name no call.
And …
Play No Ball.
No Ball. No Ball.
BY ORDER!

By kind permission of Catherine Benson. 'Play No Ball' was first published in 'The Magnificent Callisto'/Penguin Books. Gerard can be heard reading this on the 'Poetry Archive' site. He was a founder member of 'Poets on the Underground'. In 1991 he was the winner of the Signal Poetry award for his anthology 'This Poem Doesn't Rhyme'. In 1994 he was Poet-in-Residence at the Wordsworth Trust, Dove Cottage, Grasmere. Also 'In Wordsworth's Chair', 'Bradford and Beyond'/Flambard Press and 'A Good Time'/Smith Doorstop poetry anthologies.

Home Schooling Hell by Suzie Cullen

(To be sung to the tune of ABCD....)

A B C D E F G
This lesson is English – turn off the TV.
Next up maths and some chemistry
while I make lunch, dust and write my CV.
A B C D E F G
Is 10 am too early for a strong G&T?

A B C D E F G
I dream of a holiday by the sea,
a day to myself, or a shopping spree.
Home schooling's brutal – it isn't for me.
A B C D E F G
Must you come with me while I have a pee?

Suzie is a PR consultant and you can follow her on Instagram @luxebucks.

Starting Over by Clemmie Cullen

When this is all over,
I will see all my friends.
It's not the same over FaceTime
and it's really driving me round the bends.

When this is all over,
I will think in other ways,
also accept my family
and appreciate that there is more in life than just days.

When this is all over,
I will learn new things
and know to treasure my loved ones, and friends.
No one knows what this period brings.

Clemmie wrote this when she was a year 6 primary school student, aged ten, and lives in Beaconsfield, Buckinghamshire.

Give It a Chance by Jasper Cullen

During this surreal phase I am finding it tricky not being able to see friends and relatives outside my household. And I can't even go into town! But with this brings the positive of this whole situation, meaning we can get out as a family and enjoy time together. I can't wait for this to be over so we can get back to 'the norm' and then I can see friends again.

I think this affects all my friends in the same way as me (spending time with family). However, some are not fortunate to have siblings so this time could be lonely as can be! I am really thinking about my friend Adam who has lost his stepmum. But this time gives them a chance to grieve together. The family is pulling together, and this time is invaluable to make stronger bonds between us and to discover new hobbies and passions we have never tried before. We have had our first picnic in years and we have discovered a new game. We are doing 'Couch to 5k' and our grandparents are sending us quizzes.

The country is working at max capacity, especially with the amount of cases. So is the NHS. However this time prepares us better so if another outbreak were to occur, we are ready. I hope we are allowed out very soon

The world is giving itself a chance to regenerate after all the destruction and deforestation. So, we will appreciate normal life. There are a fraction of the fumes going into the air with less cars on the road, and with factories shut.

Jasper wrote this when he was a year 9 secondary student.

Life During Coronavirus by Pranshi Agarwal

In this tragic time, things have changed a lot for me. I have never been home schooled before so getting used to it was quite challenging. Friendship-wise, it is a little boring. I cannot mingle with my friends like I used to. Instead, I must rely on so much social media, even more than I used to.

All of my fun, extra-curricular activities have been cancelled (including the once-in-a-lifetime PGL trip to Georgham!) I was also supposed to go to India in the Easter holidays but as school ended early, so did all the airports. Just after school ended however, I *was* having fun, but Prime Minister Boris Johnson decided that all parks must be closed so it is the end of that story.

As it is my last year in Year 6, I will never see my primary school again (unless schools open again) and I am not sure that I am ready for the big jump to secondary school.

Not yet.

Pranshi is now a year 7 student at Dr Challoners High School. She is a keen and budding writer who loves a good old detective story. Her favourite colour is green and she absolutely hates swimming. She currently resides in Little Chalfont, Buckinghamshire with a nice toy called Cattermelon.

Sunlack Hill by Alan Halstead

On Sunlack Hill, Caesar stood.
A look of anger on his mug.
'This country is no good,' he said.
'The whole of the cohort have a cough.
There's not a centurion that isn't rough.
Pack it in, Caractacus, don't play tough.
Blow this boggy Brittanicus.
Come home, to Rome, with us.

'This country's in a real bad state.
There isn't a street that is anywhere straight.
There's not a Brit not caked in mud.
All the women are covered in woad.
No wonder our aquilifer's got an ache.
And Suetonius an upset tum.
Not a day here but the Ides of March.
Vini! Vidi! Victum!'

By kind permission of Francine Halstead. Alan was 'Rhyme & Reason's' editor 2002-2003. He obtained an MSc by research at Wadham College, Oxford 1980 and achieved Mensa membership in 1996. First published in his collection 'On Sunlack Hill'/Rhy Du Books which won 'Writing Magazine's' Self-Publishing Award. Also poetry collection 'The Poet Dines Alone'/Cherrycroft Press.

Riddle by Cailin Abercromby Gemmell

Look out, look out, one and all, whether you're big, or whether you're small.
Because I cannot be seen at all, and I won't catch you when you fall.

I multiply quickly in the heat, I travel faster than a single heartbeat.
I am far from being kind and sweet, I am not a tasty treat.

I spread like forest fires, killing every day,
I could be inside you right now, attacking you in so many ways.

I could crawl in through your mouth or ears when you're fast asleep.
Though you can't do much to stop me now, so all you can do is weep.

Don't cry in these troubled times, step up for yourself!
Volunteer for the NHS and improve sick people's health.
Don't buy everything in the store and hoard your food and wealth.

Care for the needy in these troubled times because these people need your help.
And buddy before you go, here's a tip that all of us should know:
If you want to keep me away, so you don't catch me in any way,
I suggest you wash your hands every single day!

You must do that if you touch a dirty object,
every time you have a meal or after you have been to the
toilet.
Do this every day, have a better chance of not catching me.

So this is where we part, I see, well, farewell one and all!
I hope you can figure out this little riddle.
So, our time is almost up, and I cannot tell a lie, I guess the
final words shall be ... Who am I?

*Cailin wrote this when she was nine years old and attends St
Mary's primary school in Beaconsfield, Buckinghamshire and
Stagecoach on Saturday mornings, although currently she has
ambitions to be a writer and a chef.*

What It Might Be by Christine Law

Children playing outdoors.
The chatter of happy voices.
Oh, the freedom of open gates.

No restrictions, happy
plodding through life,
with a smile on my lips,
my eyes light up.

I will shop 'till I drop
chatting to others,
going along life's happy road.
Joy and happiness to mankind.

*Christine is from Wolverhampton, West Midlands and says in
her twilight years still enjoys writing for the Rennie Grove charity.*

Teaching in Spain by Sandra Villar Otero

As a teacher it has been hard dealing with the pandemic. I live in a city called Vigo in Galicia which is in North West Spain just above Portugal. I teach in a beautiful school and the name is Alba Primary School. The pupils' ages are from 8 up to 11 years old: years 3, 4, 5 and 6. When we started the academic year in September everybody thought that after two weeks at school, children would have to go back home like they did in March. But nowadays we are all used to following the rules like using the spray to clean all the material that we manipulate and we have to leave the windows open all the time for fresh air. When it's break time each class has got its own area so children don't mix up. From my own point of view children have been fantastic and they do what they are told much better than adults. There has been something really difficult as well and it's the fact that as a friendly society we can't touch each other, hug or kiss. Hopefully this situation will change soon because mentally it's hard to cope.

Sandra is a young, single widowed mother with a fourteen-year-old daughter. Spanish is her first language.

Here we Go … by Suzie Cullen

Hickory Dickory Dock
Home schooling round the clock.
The clock strikes one
I've got nothing else done.
Pandemics and lockdowns suck.

Student Living by Olly Halton

When this is all over, I will have finished university: the last year being classes and phone calls over a pane of glass and a heap of wires. I will have left without a foot stepped in a real classroom, a book held from the library or a clasped hot chocolate by the duck pond on campus.

I'll attend coffee dates with friends, my cousin's wedding and even my own graduation. It has felt like being at sea or in deep space, far away from any person or place I can visit with only phone calls to remind me that people exist and only television programmes to show me the bustling cities of my memory.

I won't have to worry about my immune-compromised father and my sister on the other side of what feels like a war-torn country. Perhaps it is a war fought with an invisible nemesis that could be hiding in the hands of friends or clutching to the edges of our cereal boxes. In the future, I won't be saying no to any trips offered to the pub or to catch a film on a screen bigger than 65 inches, and I will hug friends tighter than before … when this is all over.

Olly is a third-year creative writing university student at the University of Winchester. Despite an additional interest in radio podcast work and journalism, his number one passion lies in fiction prose, where he is currently working on a sci-fi and fantasy novel. His website is: www.ollyhalton12.wixsite.com/ollyhaltonwrites and he has an author Twitter (www.twitter.com/OllyHalton) and Instagram (www.instagram.com/ollyhaltonwrites) accounts.

My Study Journey in Cape Town
by Kuthala Dlongwana

This is Kuthala Dlongwana, a student at the University of Western Cape (UWC) in Cape Town. Originally, I come from a small town called Cofimvaba in the Eastern Cape. I am currently busy with my degree in Education and this is my final year. I want to be a Foundation Phase teacher and develop, inspire young children from a very young age.

The year 2020 was the most challenging for me and my family, academically, financially, and emotionally as we had to adapt to new ways of doing things. At the beginning of the year when the country introduced the first 21 days of lockdown we were exposed to online learning where we had to study and attend classes from home using the technology. The Minister of Higher Education provided devices and data to participate.

However, this was not enough for some students like me to participate in this online learning as we all know that we come from different environments, different backgrounds, and different living conditions. Imagine doing online presentations, attending online classes, writing online exams in two rooms with children who are watching TV or having their own conversation. It is a challenge on its own.

It was even worse for me because I had to buy data from my own wallet in order to participate because I was provided with data for only three months. I have no idea what went wrong after; it just stopped.

On the other hand, my partner who used to sell alcohol to put bread on the table had no longer income because of the lockdown regulations.* We only survived with monthly travelling allowance money that I got from the university, which was not enough. During this period of pandemic our lives is a living hell. I just pray and hope that the year 2021 will be better, and hopefully God will hear my prayers and give plan to the presidential committee to deal with this matter effectively. *Thank you.*

The sale of alcohol was forbidden during South African lockdown periods.

Kuthala's first language is Xhosa and she lives in the township of Nyanga East, Cape Town.

Hey Ho ... by Suzie Cullen

I will *never* become a teacher. Home schooling's not for me.

Nor will I go into catering. Sod breakfast, lunch and tea!

Housekeeping is definitely *not* an option. To hell with clean and tidy.

And there's *no way* I'll become a concierge: 'Where's this? Where's that? *MUMMY!*'

Instead I'll seek some peace and quiet to soothe my lockdown frustration.

So when this quarantine is over ... you'll find me in self-isolation!

Finding Her Voice by Jude Compson

Chantal Evans loved to sing – in the shower, her bedroom, the school changing rooms. There was always some song or other playing in her head. She'd glowed when Mrs. White begged her to join the school choir, lamenting the waste of a great voice. The glow was extinguished as quickly as a snuffed-out candle when she factored in the inevitable peer-group derision.

Eventually Mrs. White's tenacity had prevailed and she'd persuaded Chantal to consider the local church girls' choir. She'd nailed the audition with a heart-felt rendition of 'Imagine'. She was surprised how welcoming the girls were. No sarcasm or mickey-taking, all just there to sing. She decided against telling her schoolmates; this was a whole new world, her world. Chantal, the girl from the council estate singing in the church choir. Sometimes she had to pinch herself.

But now nothing. The church had locked its doors over a year ago, when the first lockdown hit. Chantal felt lost, her new-found voice silent, forgotten. She prayed for this to be over and promised herself that when it was, no more hiding. She *would* join the school choir, and any other choir that would have her. Chantal Evans had to sing.

Jude lives in Hexham, Northumberland where she gardens, walks and attempts to rise to the weekly challenges set by her creative writing group tutor.

The Magic of Music by Marc Danecker

Working as a music tutor through the pandemic has been somewhat challenging, especially given that I work in schools all over and teach over a 100 students a week on a one-to-one basis. All I can say is we all learn to adapt and think up new ways to carry on. With me, it was as simple as a pull up screen which I place between myself and student. Although strange at first, everyone very quickly got used to it. The biggest struggle for me personally and financially was I couldn't open my new tuition studio, which I spent four months renovating. Thankfully we live in an age where technology can help us, as I managed to give lessons virtually online, myself sat in my studio behind my drums and the student at home behind theirs. It's not ideal but it gave us the tools to progress and move forward, plus it is kind of cool! I'm now re-opening my studio in April (2021), and thankfully the business remains strong due to the wonders of modern technology. Without that I'm not sure I would have been able to hold on to it.

I used to hate this disease, but in a strange way I'm thankful that I now know if something like this happened again, I'd be prepared for it.

Marc's tuition studio is based in Amersham, Buckinghamshire: MD MusicLab and he offers music tuition for drums, guitar, piano, vocals and much more. www.mdmusiclab.co.uk or on Facebook. He writes: 'It's a truly magical place where music rules your heart'. Marc has performed in Creative Ink's play 'Blackberry Promises' and film: 'Dear John, Dear Anyone …'

Coming up Roses by Alexa James

After 25 years of tutoring children with dyslexia, lockdown brought my working life to a pause. I spent six weeks growing roses and became so well-acquainted with the David Austin website, that a year on, I can chat quite happily about climbers to anyone prepared to listen.

'Zoom,' said a friend.

I went back to my roses.

It began to dawn on me that I would have to get my head around online teaching. The first lesson was not a success. My candidate, a lovely lad, has a slight speech impediment. We could not hear each other. We were dealing with the teaching point for 'sh' in the structured programme. I dictated the delightfully old-fashioned sentence:

'Two thrushes are nesting in the bushes.'

'Two brushes are nesting in the bushes,' he repeated.

I lay down afterwards with a cold compress.

A kind parent of one of my pupils left a silver-coloured device on my doorstep. I have no idea how Vox-Box works, but I can now hear my pupils as clear as water in a loch. It's not ideal for every child. But I love it. Will I go back to face-to-face teaching? Not on anyone's life.

Alexa is a dyslexia tutor. Many years ago she wrote articles for 'The Lady', 'Chic Chat' and for the former 'Thank God It's Friday' column of the 'Times Educational Supplement'. She is currently writing texts for children's picture books and her first children's novel. When it is all over, she hopes to escape to the West Country. She dreams of long walks, Labradors and an Aga.

Kiss by Francesca Baker

When all this is over, I'm going to kiss her. I should have kissed her as we walked merrily down the streets after one too many wines. I should have kissed her as we enveloped ourselves in literary loquaciousness, giddy on the talk of books. I should have kissed her as we sat in dark bars watching poets perform, words entrancing us and her entrancing me. Or as we walked on bright hills in the blazing sunshine, feeling the heat lick our skin, me wanting to touch her skin. I should have kissed her when she fell asleep on me on the train, her lashes quivering in hazy sleep, or when we hugged goodbye, as mates, our faces getting a bit too close.

When all this is over, I'm going to kiss her.

Francesca is a writer, reader, and word lover and writes: 'Virginia Woolf said, "My head is a hive of words that won't settle".' So she puts the words to use, exploring the world and then writing about it. You can find Francesca online at www.andsoshethinks.co.uk

Senryu by Simon Tindale

He buried his head
in the crook of his elbow
and blew her a kiss.

Guernsey's 2020 Lockdown Vision by Janet Rolfe

The other day I heard a sad, old-fashioned song. Its bluesy lyrics floated from the radio, and the words, 'Bewitched', 'Bothered' and 'Bewildered' lodged in my mind. Somehow, this gentle refrain summed up how we reacted when life in Guernsey was put on hold.

Trying to make sense of the Covid news, my husband and I stood in the front room and stared at the walls of our freshly painted prison. We were indeed bewitched – mesmerized – as if a rug had been pulled from under us; not that there were any rugs to pull, because the house was being renovated.

The word 'bothered' clearly applied. Where was our plasterer? When could the carpenter fit doors and floors? What if the boiler didn't behave?

Bewildered, we stared down the empty lane, listened in vain for the rumble of buses on the coast road. Waves prowled round the lighthouse, licked at Fort Grey's stubby tower, smashed over granite walls in Rocquaine Bay.

The familiar drone of aircraft was absent. Guernsey's yellow planes loitered by the runway; seagulls swooped in salty air. In isolation, we gazed out of the window at the island's wonderful, untouchable views.

March 2020

Born in the Channel Islands, Janet studied at the Laban Studio and Westminster College, gaining a BEd Hons from Nottingham and an MA from Loughborough during a career in Primary, Secondary and Adult Education. She studied Creative Writing at Cambridge, was awarded an MSt and is writing a family memoir of Alderney's Occupation years.

The Shape of Things to Come by Kate Moon

Thoughts from a squared-off and rectangular life – witness: the shape of every remote and screen-bound lesson I have had with my students in the past year; the shape of the keypad I am eternally pounding; the shape of the window panes looking out on to the world outside; the shape of the open books I am reading and not always finishing; the shape of the tapestry I am stitching; the shape of the screen carrying the television/films/theatre online I am watching; the shape of the ovens I am eternally filling; the shape of the seed trays I am sowing; the straight path I am walking towards the rounded edges awarded to me by: the eggs that my hens are laying; the round steering wheel guiding me to shop once a week; the wrapping of my fingers around mugs of coffee and glasses of wine and the curl of my sleeping dogs beside me on the sofa – all Squaring the Circle until we're free.

Kate – once a BBC voice – segued to voice and presenter agent for over 30 years – segued to now as voice coach and teacher in the rural climes of Northamptonshire.

Pause Rap by Catherine Klyhn

So called 'living' in a shocked town
silence feels like we might drown
sidestepping contamination
eerily empty underground station
rusty old bikes kick into action
random drivers irked by distraction
children caged in sanitized spaces
limited to 5 K in familiar places
exhausted dogs flop languidly
humans keen 'cos walks are handy
shelves with loose limbs no longer laden.
Amazon? But where is it 'made in'?
Eagerly awaiting the day
when we can Replay, Replay, Replay.

And ... Pause.

Catherine emigrated from Ireland in the 1980s and worked in the City for nearly 20 years. She's now a full-time mum and volunteer. She is a Creative Inker and hosted many Creative Ink evening workshops.

Perfect Symbiosis by Geraldine Newbrook

Early lockdown, an early walk. Through the village and into the churchyard. There, standing in its own quiet space was a little tree, its first blossoms catching the light. Close by, two ancient headstones – dates and details long worn away – leaned in. Young tree, old bones: perfect symbiosis, the little tree guarding those sleeping below whose remains I fancied were still nourishing the tree as it kept watch over them. A small circle of life in an English country churchyard whose story I just had to paint.

It turned out that my contribution was just to sit at my easel. The picture all but painted itself: the little tree taking centre stage with no regard for any artistic rules. Much shown was true: the tree, the headstones, the old stone wall, the bluebells; but the stream just happened to wander through on its own. Yet another reminder of continuance …

Of course, the graves will weather even more and the little tree will itself grow old, its branches becoming less strong, its blossoms less dense and sweet. But elsewhere, in similar sacred places, where other dear ones rest in peace, other trees will stand sentry duty and other streams will pass through, singing, as bluebells ring out yet another of Spring Time's Great Round. World without end.

Geraldine is 80, married 60 years in June, two grown-up children, four live grandchildren. Likes painting, travelling and has more books to read than years left to live.

A Walk in the Woods by Aaron Eames

I went walking in the woods today
for my hour-long recreation;
every animal kept away
per government recommendation.

All I got was a silent look
from a ruffled, old wood pigeon;
I tried to chat to a babbling brook
but I couldn't get a word in.

A woman, doggedly jogging,
paused to let me by;
neither of us said a thing,
I couldn't tell you why.

In these days of quarantine
normal life seems strange.
But it's quite reassuring
very little has changed.
8th April 2020

Aaron has an MSt in Creative Writing from the University of Cambridge and is a PhD student at Loughborough University. He comes from the village of Whitwick in Leicestershire (neither of which are pronounced how they're spelt).

Walking Alone by Sasha Morris

Walking alone out in the rain,
a busy road or a quiet lane.
Avoiding dogs with muddy paws
who are flouting the social distancing laws.
No conversation,
but birdsongs rule.
No commuting or journey to school.
Follow a daily familiar way,
step by step and day by day.

Are there truly some positives here?
The environment thanks you,
the air's more clear.
White feathers and wildflowers light the track.
The trail's the same.
and now turn back.
The rain will fall; the sun will shine.
I'm not afraid when I get back home,
but the fact remains
I'm on my own.
March 2020.

Sasha writes that she was recently widowed and was just getting used to living on her own when the pandemic struck.

The Wood at Pucks Paigles by Christopher North

An April storm of blue.
A lake's deep swarm
of blue blue,
pure blue
newly arrived.

Newly found blue,
not sky blue,
but woodland's blue,
new in drifts.

A cloud rush
stream of blue.
A water ground
blue on green,
million specked
beneath beech splay,
bluescape.

Within the woodland nave
blue armies of dusk,
blue bloom on green spears,
blue platoons
spread, penetrate.

And the sheaves of blue,
harvest sheaves
thick in gathered blueness.
And above all
not 'Lad's Love's dim avenue'

but a scent
of woodland upon woodland
in all the places of woodland,
to childhood's blue distance.

No poppy here,
no yellow rape,
spurge green
or garlic white.
This blue.
This spread wide flood of blue,
scent of gloom blue,
green blue,
blue blue.

Originally from Little Chalfont, Buckinghamshire, Christopher and his wife now live in a Spanish mountain village near Alicante, Spain where in a converted olive mill he and his wife offer writing retreats www.oldolivepress.com. He has three full collections published (Oversteps Books) and three pamphlets. The latest 'The Topiary of Passchendaele'/Smith Doorstop was launched at the Wordsworth Centre in Grasmere in 2018. His first pamphlet (also Smith Doorstop) 'A Mesh of Wires' was shortlisted for the Forward Prize in 1999.

Locked Down in Liverpool by Angela Cheveau

Terraced houses, brazen beneath the sky. Bricks slapped bright with sunlight, huddle like gossiping ladies in old school hairnets. Chimney pot shadows face each other like lovers about to kiss. Bees pollen drunk, sway between unruly purple flowers that spill on to pavements, bruising the street with their purple haze. Whispered wishes flutter amongst freshly washed clothes flapping on lines like strings of bright prayer flags. Wheelie bins stand sentry in alleyways while weeds gasp for air, struggling through choking concrete.

Life is hard here. You need tough bones. Poverty etches itself on to faces of people who can't find the money to feed open-mouthed children. The hard face of a once proud city brought to its knees. The distant wail of sirens is a sound track played on repeat. A sequin rainbow throws thanks to the girl in the mask. Shoulders bowed, heavy with the weight of duty, she enters houses folding her wings around the old, lonely and sick. A man walks down the street, hands in pockets, his dreams emptying on to the pavement like loose change. Above, the sun weaves a golden trail across the sky. A seagull takes flight, feathers dipped in gold.

Nobody notices.

Angela is featured in two upcoming anthologies with a writing charity called Writing on the Wall in Liverpool and has a short piece published on the 'Women on Writing' blog as part of their Friday 'Speak Out' Section.

Tesco – Monday Morning – April 2020 by Sue Johnson

A familiar place and time made strange by current events. We are social distancing across the car park waiting to be allowed inside. We follow the arrows, glance furtively at each other. Someone jokes about having a singalong. He indicates the blackbird singing amongst the fresh green leaves. Far away in London the prime minister is in hospital fighting for his life. I enter the store, fill my trolley remembering to give thanks for all that I have. Try to push back the tide of worry that rises inside me when I think of those I love.

Sue is a poet, novelist and creative writing tutor based in Evesham, Worcestershire. Further details of her work can be found at www.writers-toolkit.co.uk

Spring by William Ivens

Escape to the wild woods where striking bursts
of azalea and rhododendron explode
in secret corners.
Trace the undulating flight of tits meandering
through glade and shimmering shadow.

Wisteria begins to pale and droop
as brilliant yellow mimosa pendant
brightens the spirit.
Beech trees so recently entirely naked
now rejoice in full, tender green.

Roses promise as lavender sprouts flower
and buttercups bid welcome with embracing petal.
Freshly mown grass stimulates the nose
as horses clop their effortless rhythm.

Nestlings chirp and insects swarm –
an opera of natural magic.
People walk, keeping their distance
but always with a warming smile.

William has been retired now for nearly six years. He has lived in Buckinghamshire for over 30 years, the last 5 in Seer Green – a village outside Beaconsfield. He potters in the garden, watches sport, reads and would normally enjoy eating and drinking out and socializing. He sold metal to the aircraft industry for most of his career, and, in his youth ran his own mobile discotheque.

Give or Take by John Ling

It was a testing time.
Of how much and how little.
Of how much we could take
and how much we had taken.
How little we had given.
Of how much give and take
we could bear with.
Bear with us, they said.
It will take time.
How much? we said.
Too much, we felt.
This much, they said, perhaps.
Another said, that much, maybe.

And Earth said, not enough.
You've had your chance.
Now it's my turn.

John is a mediator for kids with special needs and angry neighbours. Facilitator of AVP workshops (Alternatives to Violence Project) for people who can't handle conflict.

Virus Lockdown, Week 1 by Moyra Zaman.

Spring smiles
a warm glow, framed
frosty at the edges,
watching our confinement
unfold, in various
backyards.

I watch the great tits
tickle the lavender and
peck the boughs,
oblivious, it seems,
of freedoms lost, humanity
poised hesitantly.

As I try to remember
her name, my neighbour
bursts into song –
an aria, no less, controlled
yet soaring effortlessly,
as the birds fly.

Her voice, only known
in 'good girl' pronouncements,
training a Christmas pup,
defied restraint, emerging
secretly from silence,
a gifted gem.

This soul could soothe
congested lungs, listening in

forgotten corridors, death's
distraction … yet, notes quiver,
words go viral, as I hear her
coughing into the night.

*Moyra is a mother and grandmother from Amersham,
Buckinghamshire, a world traveller, retired art teacher of twenty
years, formerly a biochemist, now a part-time yoga teacher and a
volunteer trustee of Workaid who enjoys writing.*

Daisy Days by Louise Norton

A small plump child's hand grabs a fine daisy,
thrilled with wonder on spying dear flower.
Sun touches rosy cheeks, hair a-wavy.
Buttercups and dandelions, all ours,
cartwheels, handstands in magical meadows,
tumbling, running, leapfrog, favourite friends.
Long days reaching the sky, silky breeze blows,
sit in circles, daisy chains with no ends.
Squeals of merriment singing in the sun,
the garden pond where creepy crawlies grow.
Eager mouths licking ice cream on the run …
Fairies and tadpoles, lupins in a row.
My hand wrinkled and worn picks new daisies,
same feelings inside, outside … old lady.

*Louise is an ex-professional dancer/choreographer from
Glasgow, Scotland and still exploring the wonders of life. She
enjoys playing with song and dance and with words.*

First Lockdown from Suburbia *by Christina Blake*

We hasten to the evergreen.
Sweet nature are you there?
Bucolic vistas fill our thoughts,
we've time to stand and stare.

Footpaths forking right and left
but which best to disclaim?
And as in life, we'll never know
'less we pass this way again.

Proverbial coin is tossed and on
to destiny unknown,
we tread the dusty pathway
which leads away from home.

Toeing fields with mewling sheep
and hedgerows hiding clover.
Skies swept clear of crochet clouds
full crystal blue high over.

We've learnt the poem, feigned the art
but left the poor muse crying.
The life we had when we didn't care
alas is slowly dying.

The highway ribbon smooth and sleek
still cruising into town.
No takers for its accuracy
while cars are in lockdown.

Eyes peer out above a mask
and plead do see me too,
while feet away from words and touch
all sadly now taboo.

Old folk wait for kith and kin
to feel their touch again.
Not daring to allow the thought
that living is in vain.

They wipe away their loneliness
as they wipe away their tears.
Their old life just a memory
now catalogued in years.

Christina writes that she made the most of chances she had and made chances where there were none. She is now living in Buckinghamshire with her husband and dog: free from the constraints of work and ambition. Free to be whimsical, spontaneous, gregarious, creative, lazy and … a grandma to be.

Ravens in Lockdown by Terry Gifford

There's a frost melting on the Mendip meadows
as I drive into sunrise for the last time this spring.
In the grass patch of the quarry tiny yellow heads
have been burned by ice in May. It's all change
here, at six-twenty, when I round the corner to see
that last youngster on the rim above the nest,
freed of overhanging rock, awaiting a feed.

Each year, the young family assemble on the south
rim where the other three now waddle into sight.
There's a secret source of worms, and perhaps even
afterbirth, behind the trees of the west end
from where the adults fly to feed these juveniles.
The arching cloudless firmament is egg-blue
for their fledged future in the new normal.
12 May 2020

Twelfth dawn visit to this locked, disused, Somerset quarry to make a nest record: an annual activity.

As Visiting Research Fellow at Bath Spa University's Research Centre for Environmental Humanities, Terry gives guest lectures on MA programmes, including the MA Travel and Nature Writing, directed by the ornithologist and nature writer Stephen Moss. Terry lives in Wookey, outside Wells, Somerset. His eighth collection is 'A Feast of Fools'/Cinnamon Press, 2018. www.terrygifford.co.uk

The Others by Kat Frend

A cloudless sky, a soundless street
a peaceful retreat
trying not to think of the others.

Cleaning the sink, clearing the weeds
growing new seeds
trying not to think of the others.

Teaching kids to bake, zooming friends,
making cheerful cards to send
trying not to think of the others.

Hearing the birdsongs, smelling the lilacs
finding new walking tracks
trying not to think of the others.

Turning off the news, hugging yourself
checking your health
thinking and thinking of all the others.

Kat is 47 and from Buckinghamshire, UK.

I Am Me by Chloe Lambert

Right now …
I am here …
This is the here and now …
I see every sunrise and every sunset …
Here I stand …
I am me …

I am here …
I can see the trees …
I can feel the breeze …
Here I stand …
I am me …

I am here …
I am enough …
It is okay to be me …
me …
Here I stand …
I am me …

I am here …
I can see the stars and the moon …
I can see the flowers sway …
Here I stand …
I am me …

I feel the rain and the cold …
I feel the warmth of the sun …
I have a voice …
Hear me …

See me …

Hear. I stand …
I am me.

Chloe has lived in Cornwall for five years. She was a primary school teacher and is now working as a teaching assistant.

Yo! Boomer by Lucy Skelton

Yo! Boomer, get back indoors.
Don't tell us this is only flu.
Don't tell us that Boris will get this sorted.

Yo! Boomer, you voted for the arrogant blond.
Voted to crush the nurses.
Voted in a brutal future.

Voted for isolation – how ironic now.

Lucy is a middle-aged woman living a middle class life in Buckinghamshire. Originally from London via Bangkok.

New Vocabulary by Pippa Hawkins

The Curve:
a graph that builds
reaches a frightening point.
I ache for those who cannot say
goodbye.

Lockdown
has no jailer
but is dinners alone,
packs of cyclists around the lake,
a siege.

Covid
travels quickly,
creates fear – my stomach's
acid rush with each announcement
panic.

Screening
has no popcorn,
no late-night cinema
just an attempt to contain the
terror.

Social
Distancing – a
line that measures love in
metres, the space between feels like
torture.

Pippa retired from her work as an FE lecturer to write poetry. She was awarded a Masters in Creative Writing at Swansea University. Her pamphlet 'The Care Line'/Cinnamon Press 2018 collects some of her poems about caring for her husband. She enjoys sharing poetry in a number of groups in Bristol.

The Herd by Jane Edmonds

One raised head, a stamp of hoof,
the panic spreads, they're on the move;
a scampering wave, white scuts of fear
flashing a signal: get out of here!
One stops to snatch a tuft of grass,
then many stop so none can pass.
Furred ears are twitching back and forth
catching sounds of threatened death:
a leaping surge, a scattered dash
leaves behind bloodied mortal flesh.
March 2020

Jane has lived in Beaconsfield, Buckinghamshire for the last 27 years and before that in various parts of Britain and the world. She co-runs 'Poetry that Pleases' and attends a writers' group, both initiated by Quakers. She is currently undertaking a creative writing degree with the Open College of the Arts.

The Current Situation by Bryn Strudwick

The lighting failed on Thursday
and I didn't know what to do.
So I rang an ELECTRICIAN
to see WATT he could do.

His response wasn't very POSITIVE
in the CURRENT situation.
He'd decided to go to EARTH
and stay OHM in INSULATION.

He still got LIGHT exercise daily
with a SHORT CIRCUIT round the park,
but he couldn't come to visit me:
I'd just have to stay in the dark.

Although I begged him to help me
he put up STRONG RESISTANCE.
He was following government GRIDLINES
And keeping his SOCIAL DISTANCE.

I tried to PYLON the agony
Pleading old age in the MAIN,
but his answer was in the NEGATIVE
and don't CONTACT him again.

He said I'd have to do it myself
I really wasn't amused.
He said it wasn't his VOLT.
He refused, so I RE-FUSED.

Bryn was born in Enfield but now lives in Basingstoke, Hampshire and has been writing for more than 70 years.

Stuck Inside by Andrew Mason

Fate throws a stick and most wail and dive for cover; we hide away and fear the fear. We feel cold and anxious at staying too long in the company of our own thoughts. We shudder at the loss to our cozy pile of coins and stand aghast at the changes wrought on routine, order and complacent sleep.

For every painful tear, a drop of rain to succour. For every passing, a beginning; this is as ever has been. Turn your head and sense the calm that comes with pause. Breathe inward silence; inhale your own vitality. Taste the survival spirit of eons past and ages future. That is all.

Isolation is its own reward; you are a thousand selves inside you and you are a sentient being, capable of incredible adaptation to your environment. You have memory, imagination and inner tranquility to offer other worlds to visit. I hope everybody turns their head.

Andrew is an 'Amershaman' – Buckinghamshire. An ageing traveller who comes from the memories inside him, perhaps? He writes: 'Certainly, my only reality of self and of home now travel quietly within me'.

Once in a Hundred Years by Janice Braysher

Cruise cabin quarantine. Stranded citizens. Novel virus doesn't discriminate. Fever. Or new, persistent cough (catch it, bin it). Wash hands. Soap and hot water. Sing 'Happy Birthday' twice. Physical distancing two metres apart. Self-isolate. Panic buying. Over 70s and underlying health conditions. Shielding three to eighteen months. Herd immunity. Informed by the science. Daily updates. Confirmed cases. Deaths. Stay home. Protect the NHS. Save lives. Global economic crash. Lockdown. One hour exercise. Essential shopping. Emergency travel. Key work. Clap for Carers – not enough PPE, not enough testing, not enough ventilators. No health system could cope. Waves. Flatten the curve. Pass the peak. Suppress R below 1. Race for a vaccine. Big Brother is watching. Engage. Explain. Encourage. Enforce: stay safe. Protect the NHS. Save lives.

Currently in Ayrshire, Scotland, Janice is by nature nomadic which feeds her writing; she has had success with short pieces and is working on her novel.

Haiku for Troubled Times by Maureen Boon

Take **C**are **O**f yourself.
Visualise an **I**deal world.
Don't give up, stay strong!

Maureen writes children's stories, short stories and flash fiction and lives in the lovely Devon countryside near Chudleigh.

2020 and On by Tom Harrison

When this is all over, I'll need a four leaf clover, dinghies in Dover, a troubling sarcoma. This is life, trouble and strife. Trying to thrive, staying alive, another dollar, another day, clock on, clock off. Despair, repair, breakdown, breakthrough. Waxing, waning, constantly explaining. Funeral casks, families in masks, through the looking glass. Pain, shame, HS2 gravy train. Isolation, frustration, Earth's continuing gyration. Impending doom, gathering gloom, grand mal seizure, bodies in the freezer. A pair of jays, the sun's rays, a boiler steaming, a child screaming. Chilblain, Dunblane, peg tooth, thatched roof. Over the side, slippery slide, Flying Dumbo, Lieutenant Columbo. Hubble Bubble, Toil and Stubble. Burning Books, unemployed cooks, dirty looks, billhooks. Grow Up. Eat Up. Put up or shut up. High Street. Police Beat. Giving up Meat. Did I tell you I was vegan?

Thunberg's Iceberg. Messianic. Titanic. IMF. IVF. HTF. A man called Geoff. Cleft palate. Timmy Mallett. Feeling sick. Tom Dick. Roaring Twenties, British strawberries, overflowing cemeteries. Please check your testes. Solar Farms. Polar Harms. Electric cars. Man on Mars. Hug and hate, you're my mate. Don't forget to close the gate. Fireside chats, nipping gnats, won't you try these sprats?

This is over, Mr Bolsover.

Tom comes from Mother Nature and will return there in due course. He is from Amersham, Buckinghamshire and suffered a seizure during 2020 when Humanity was looking out for him as a GP was passing and saved his life.

Erasure by Jill Wilkinson

When the rainbow pictures have gone and those chalked on pavements washed away, what else will be erased from our lives? Supermarket deliveries? Frustratingly difficult to find a slot at first and menu planning was a race against sell-by dates. Substitutions were amusing: when no cucumbers were available they sent a courgette!

The family get-together on Zoom? Defined by pictures disappearing, sound breaking up and everyone talking at once. 'I can see you but can't hear you … now I just have the top of your head.' Masks and gloves? Basic weapons in our armoury. We soldiered on with steamed up glasses, struggling to hear each other's muffled voices. Then battling with gloves, when removing them, they refused to leave our fingers.

Will the new words and phrases disappear or stay with us? Lockdown, self-isolating, social distancing, the new normal, stay safe and extraordinary times. Perhaps some things will remain. Working from home, many rediscovered the pleasure of cooking and found benefits to mental health from gardening. Daily outdoor exercise kindled an interest in the natural world and hopefully sparked a determination to live *with* nature, not dominate and abuse it. Will this new found appreciation change the world?

Originally from Nottinghamshire and now living in Hampshire to be close to family, Jill is a 74-year-old granny who loves nature and the countryside.

Sing a Song by Fiona Gibbs

Sing a song of pangolin,
a pocket full of lies.
Four and twenty Asian bats
baked in a pie.
When the pie was opened,
the bats began to sing;
Oh, wasn't that a dainty dish
to set before a king?

The king was in his counting house,
counting out the deaths.
The queen was in the castle,
swigging down the meths.
The maid was in the garden,
hanging out the clothes;
along came coronavirus
and snuffled up her nose.
April 2020

Fiona is from Great Missenden, Buckinghamshire and joined Creative Ink classes a while back. She lives with a husband from Sri Lanka and a hormonal dog from Lithuania. She has two adult sons who now live under Tier 2 lockdown.

Sounds in the Air by Margaret Gregory

Spring petals fall in the rustling breeze.
A black bird sings from its lofty perch.
Another replies, perhaps competes,
each song so intricate, so diverse
until a faint wail becomes a scream.
The siren's shriek slices through the air.
Its brutal top note strangles our breath.
But now it's gone, bearing life or death.
Stillness returns, though tension remains,
as we think of those crying in pain
and the trusted hands that bring them ease.

Margaret has lived in England for most of her life, though she was born in America.

Joggers and Road Hoggers by Suzie Cullen

Won't give way to an elderly stranger.
You're hoggers – you joggers.
My daily walk's fraught with danger.
There's no law against hogging – no sentence nor flogging
to punish your selfish ways.
But please I implore … Give Way! Don't ignore
us older lot on our one walk a day.
We are no longer so agile.
Some of us fragile,
in one piece we'd like to stay!

On Reflection by Hilary Frend

Silence, as the saying goes, is golden. No traffic hurtling past and no helicopter or plane in the bright blue sky. A truly peaceful time. Lockdown has been a chance for everyone to slow down and appreciate nature in all its glory. On daily walks, to see beautiful trees in a vast array of greens, the flowers and all the busy bees. To watch birds flying in a clear sky and listen to their songs. Old and young may have seen all this and have felt the benefit. It has been a time for nature to come to the fore.

This strange time has made people relax and take stock of their lives. Not being able to see family and friends has reminded people of *important* things. A smile, a laugh, a hug. Being kind and caring to those you know and do not. It is usually the little things which give special meaning to our lives. In years to come, in busy lives once more, hopefully people will remember this calmer time, to appreciate that it has been special in many ways.

Hilary is a positive fun-loving grandmother in her early 70s from Buckinghamshire.

Haiku by Hugh Hodge

Silence follows him
as the wake follows the ship
and the albatross.

Hugh is a baby boomer brat. Born in England, arrived in SA as an infant. He has edited SA's 'Contrast' magazine and has run Cape Town's 'Off the Wall' readings.

What I Will Do ... by Hilary Bates

I will have …

Hair like Marc Bolan.
A taste for hippy clothes.
Psychedelic face masks.
Corns on my toes.

I will have …

Worn out my trainers.
Lost half a stone.
Alienated my neighbours
by playing the trombone.

I will have …

Cleaned every corner.
Polished all the chrome.
Fancy new curtains
in a clutter-free home.

I will have …

Cracked the Times crossword.
Gorged on Mills and Boon.
Clapped every Thursday.
Learnt how to zoom.

I will have …

Been on a bear hunt.
Taught myself Walloon.
Knitted a rainbow.
Seen a pink moon.

I will have …

Forgotten about Brexit.
Found an old friend.
Remembered what's important:
love wins in the end.
April 2020

Hilary is a semi-retired Francophile living in Bedfordshire.

Super Moon by Helen Nicell

Here I sit in isolation, super moon at its height.
Shadows cast a magical glow, bathing garden in pools of white.
Clouds weave a mackerel sky, scales parting to reveal the moon.
Nowhere to go, no plans made, for now, home is a safety cocoon.
I can sleep late tomorrow, absorbing nature and behold
nocturnal activity in the garden: foxes wander red and bold
weaving across the path, eerie light shows their route
off to the dense woodland, silent night, the world on mute.

A virus has made us all stand still to appreciate warm spring days.
Tulips and daffodils nod in the sun, hyacinth borders, colours ablaze.
Aircraft grounded leaving clear blue sky, peace without the motorway hum.
Birdsong louder and clearer, fresh air filling heart and lung.
No deadlines, no appointments, talk with daughters and sons.
Not in person, but via a screen, telling people, they are our loved ones.
Think of the things that matter the most, this time will pass all too soon.
Embrace the enforced isolation and take time to look at the moon.

Helen joined Watford Writers in Hertfordshire fifteen years ago. She has produced over a 100 short stories and poems. She now co-runs the group which has been meeting weekly online since March 2020.
www.watfordwriters.org

Taking a Risk by Alexa James

The NHS letter states that I am 'at very high risk'. I refer to my consultant's letter in summer 2019, suggesting I have a trial without immune suppressive medication. I've learnt over the years to say 'no'. In summer 2019, I refused to stop taking the medication to see if I have a natural remission. Now seems the time to try my rheumatologist's experiment.

I find myself on a balmy April evening, several weeks without medication staring at my feet. Is there swelling in my ankle? I consult with my husband. Although blessed with a science background, he is as incapable as I am of identifying inflammation. We peer not only at my feet, but his too. We make comparisons. His feet seem remarkably similar to mine. I wonder about a photo, taking a little medication and doing a 'before' and 'after' comparison. What about a blood test? But do I want to take the risk with Covid circulating?

'Leave it another week and then inject?' he hazards.

I concur.

Hatred is not my scene. And I mean that. Honestly. He helps me with my socks. 'I loathe the Chinese Communist Party,' I say.

And I mean that. Honestly.

April 2020

For the Earth by Michelle Gunner

Our life on hold, the earth breathes.

The curtain of pollution lifts
and skies dazzle.
On the dark velvet robe of night
jewels sparkle
and from afar a child sees a star
for the very first time.

Life on hold, the earth breathes.

Cities are deserted,
the heaving mass of people has vanished.
Ships have ceased from pouring filth.
In seas, canals and rivers
fish frolic in transparent waters.
Only the scent of flowers perfumes the air.
The roar of planes has died away
leaving birds' songs to enchant our day.

A malevolent magician has cursed mankind:
serendipity for the earth which breathes
while our life is on hold.

Michelle is a Parisenne poet whose first language is French.
She was Business Manager (1994) and an editor of 'Rhyme &
Reason' (1995). She is a long-standing member of Metroland

Poets, author of the novel 'An Orchid in Winter' and poetry collection 'Collages'/New Generation Publishing and available on Amazon.

Tax by Alan Halstead

I am not normally suicidal
and claim to be passingly mathematical.
But this year's income tax revenue guide
is absolutely, shambolically, diabolical.

First published in Alan's collection 'On Sunlack Hill'/Rhy Du Books.

SUMMER

'OUR SUMMER SALAD DAYS …'

SHAKESPEARE'S 'ANTHONY AND CLEOPATRA'

Ode to the 1905 Salad by Lorri Nicholson

We sat on a porch,
in the comfortable shade of forever,
and drank glistening pitchers of ice-cold Sangria,
fruit flush with red wine;
the waiter rolled his r's,
jamar –
eat –
he would say in a Cuban Spanish,
preparing the salad at the table
like an absolution.

In 1905,
in Tampa Bay's Ybor city,
the salad was served on brash,
yellow and blue Cuban crockery,
rimmed in the orange of a Florida sunrise,
(not a sunset which is a paler hue)
and topped with great-green Spanish olives.
No words were used to name the salad,
as if English were not up to the job.

In the thirties, they rolled cigars,
and drank thick brown Cuban coffee.
In the fifties, the rooms filled with smoky music,
and the tang of black beans and rice.
In the seventies they read Neruda in Spanish,
questions written in a green pen of hope,
and looked for themselves pronounced
in the language.

In 2020,
the world shrank,
and everyone ate off white plates.

Today,
I roll r's along my tongue,
and practise the glorious trill
of pronunciations:
good words
I pick up like little rocks
and skim across the water,
through time like fossils.

Lorri is an American married to a Geordie. She lived in Northumberland for several years, and moved back to Virginia, America just in time for the lockdown. She used to live in Florida, and this poem is the musings of one who cannot travel or go to restaurants.

How to Cook a Haiku by Jan Moran Neil

Place idea in pan.
Gently simmer. Bring to boil.
Haiku in minutes.

First published in Jan's collection 'Serving Bluebird Pie'/ Creative Ink Publishing.

The Penguin Book of Mediterranean Food
by Catherine Benson

Spine faded, pages yellowed, corners turned down
for the recipes she'd wished she could afford.
Whole menus of wishing.

On the list of contents an oil-stained receipt
needs peeling off the page. The Deli, Blackheath.
Now the prices seem so low, but back then …
The Chianti in a basket, sour to her tongue, which became
a candle-holder dripped with wax, like Vesuvius,
and took a ¼ or more of her week's housekeeping.

The receipt was meant to be a memento
of the anniversary meal, scrimped for. Instead
she remembers how late he was. That's when it all began.
Night after night. She screws up the bit of memory.
How she thought to reach his heart. Hoped
to find it where the cliché said she would. Remembers

the honey Soraya Bread, hours taken to thicken cream
over a slow heat until thick enough to roll, slice
and put on top of each cut square. Hours taken.
Remembers the time it took to pound the meat flat,
thin strips sautéed, still pink, then garlic-creamed.
The intricate placing of colours in the salad.

The sophistication of the starter, crudités. Her own dips.
The card she'd made. The baby well-fed, asleep.
And centre table, the single rose she's bought. One candle.

First published in the 'Rialto' magazine and was used to promote the magazine at the Norwich Festival. Catherine is a poet and an illustrator, illustrating many of her husband Gerard's poems for children.

Where Have All the Flours Gone? by Regina Simpson

Long time passing …
Where have all the flours gone?
Lockdown bakers have picked them every one.
When will we ever learn?
Hoarding is a great concern.

Regina (Reggie) is a transplanted American long living in the UK. Her essay 'Do not count the days; make the days count' was published in the 'Rhyme & Reason' Freedom 2018 diary (to coincide with World Alzheimer's Day). Reggie writes: 'Disability has left me living in splendid self-isolation long before Covid, but the brain remains sharp'.

Variety Is the Spice by Linda Storey
(For John Clarence More)

My father told me stories of his childhood in India. He was born in 1910 in Allahabad, situated on the River Ganges, to British parents where his father worked for the government. My grandmother and her children moved to the cooler and fresher climate of the Kumaon Hills, in the foothills of the Himalayas, for their education.

He died in 1986 in London. We sorted through his belongings, painful for my mother, but for me the pain was eased by an excitement as I uncovered notebooks and folded pieces of paper full of recipes for curries, Indian breads, chutneys and pickles. Words like aloo, muttar, dahl, khichari, and chapattis sprung out of the pages, reminiscent of his past.

Dad had left a legacy. These scruffy, stained, hand-written recipes written in his own childish hand with spelling mistakes were mine. Foods he had prepared at our London home that I had eaten, enjoyed, hated, remembering the burning, fiery sensation around my lips and tongue. I needed more. The life he once lived had resulted in the suggestion of something exotic from a distant world that had somehow become a part of our daily bread.

My daughter's request for early family photos took me to a long-hidden box in the loft where I uncovered Dad's little books and curry-stained bits of paper.

GREEN CHUTNEY
50g fresh mint leaves
25g fresh coriander leaves
Garlic

Slice of onion
1 green chilli
Dessertspoon raw pistachios
Pinch dried mango powder
Lemon juice
30ml water
Purée all together and store in screw top jar in fridge. Serve with grilled Indian meats and bread.

Linda is a Londoner, now living in Beaconsfield, Buckinghamshire. She is retired and enjoys creative art in all forms, both physical and emotional. She writes: 'Now is the time to feature these recipes in my father's biography'.

The Trolley Dance by Paul Stephen

A new landscape is born,
from this sweeping tide of
change and manipulation.
The crab dance of avoidance
in the local shop, two metres apart,
our mouths closed and eyes blank.
Masks cover our sins, no smiles
at the trolley dance.

Paul is from Leeds. His day job is working in the HR office for Northern Rail but he enjoys following a shamanic life and teaches Reiki when restrictions allow. He loves poetry and the economical use of words to convey a feeling and thought.

Covid in Snehalaya, India by Nick Cox

My beautiful niece Amber used to make regular sojourns to a yoga retreat in Goa and I kept promising I'd make the trip with her one day. When Amber lost her brave battle to cancer it was her dad's wish to have her ashes scattered where she had been most at peace. After successfully doing this I embarked on a journey that would change my life forever. It began when I met a young lady on a crowded bus who told me she'd just finished volunteering at Snehalaya: a shelter home for women and children rescued from slum and red light areas. I wanted to know more about them.

My first time at Snehalaya was to deliver funds I'd raised on behalf of my family and friends. I was shown around their various projects and I particularly connected to the work they were doing in the fields of domestic violence and HIV. I lost many friends and work colleagues to AIDS-related illnesses. I was blown away by what Snehalaya was achieving in the areas of prevention, education and awareness. The various roles I play here include: honorary director, making short documentaries, volunteer management, working with a fundraising team and giving presentations all over the country.

I live in their Rehabilitation Centre with around 300 people. Many of the kids here are children of sex workers and have inherited the HIV virus. When the pandemic first struck India, it was terrifying to think how vulnerable people in the slum areas were living in such close proximity. Snehalaya started a strict no one in, no one out policy and so far it's served us well. We are lucky residing here in our bubble but as you know it just takes one prick to burst it. It's a constant fear.

When this is all over I will explore new and familiar territories.

Addendum: May 2021. Have run out of beds in hospitals, vaccines, equipment. Staff and children here in quarantine. Am staying.

Nick did two seasons at the National Youth Theatre where, he writes: 'I met a certain young lady called Jan Moran Neil née Titterington'. Nick went on to work extensively in theatre and television, including 'Doctor Who' and the Saturday morning live TV show 'No 73' alongside Sandi Toksvig.

Local Heroes by Barbara Pavey

This morning I was at a local Farmers' and Crafts' Market. At the cheese stall a lovely young lady was serving. She was okay when someone wanted to pay by card, but a little flummoxed with the cash side of things and how to count out the correct change. She stated apologetically that she had learning difficulties. I looked around at how different everything now was for all of us: veiled faces, one-way systems, social distancing, regular hand sanitizing – I guess we all battle with learning difficulties until we've mastered the new norm, which by the way, is ever changing. Instead of seeing her 'weakness' I saw someone with a lovely smile, standing for a long time in hot and sticky conditions, politely serving others to the best of her ability.

She taught *me* something today.

Barbara is a former student of Creative Ink and lives in Buckinghamshire. She enjoys writing, languages, travelling, theatre, eating out, Nordic walking, driving, socializing, and exploring her Christian faith.

Marlene Dietrich's Banana Bread by Jenny Hammerton

Marlene Dietrich may strike you as a movie star who wouldn't be seen dead in an apron but on the contrary, she loved to cook. Many folks took up the baking of banana bread to soothe their souls during the pandemic. If you fancy sprinkling some stardust around your kitchen with a tinsel town recipe, here's Marlene's very own way of making this sweet treat.

Marlene Dietrich's Banana Nut Bread

200g plain flour
¾ teaspoon bicarbonate of soda
1¼ teaspoons cream of tartar
½ teaspoon salt
75g butter
150g caster sugar
2 eggs
1 cup mashed banana pulp (about 2½ bananas)
75g finely chopped walnuts

Preheat oven to 180°C.

Sift flour with bicarbonate of soda, cream of tartar and salt. In another bowl, cream the butter and add the sugar gradually, mix until light and fluffy. Add the eggs, one at a time, beating well after each addition. Add the dry ingredients alternately with banana pulp and beat the mixture until thoroughly combined; then add the chopped walnuts and mix through. Pour into a well-greased loaf pan (10cmx23cmx7.5cm); bake for one hour or until done.

Jenny has been eating like her movie star idols and writing about their favourite recipes for over fifteen years. You can read about her triumphs and failures over at www.silverscreensuppers.com

Ode to Wallace and Gromit by David Halstead

We're trying to kill off this disease
with hard work and some great expertise
but up in the Dales
there's encouraging tales
that it succumbs to Wensleydale cheese.

David was born and brought up in West Yorkshire with a belated sense of wanting to help others and a keen sense of humour. He writes: 'You would need this if you were born and brought up in West Yorkshire'.

Prime Time by Regina Simpson

If ever a company's got its business model right
Amazon's the one.
Lockdown and retail therapy.
And now Amazon Fresh, free to Prime members like me:
groceries next day delivered, delivery free!
Future lockdown at speed. Supermarkets take heed.

Slim Times by Fiona Lyons

The first lockdown shook the nation. Locked up in our homes with nothing to do. The days seemed endless with no end of this in sight. It was a novelty at first but then it dragged on. What was there to do? FaceTimes with friends and family, the odd walk here and there just to get out the house, binge watching TV series you wouldn't have dreamt of watching whilst mindlessly eating the contents of the cupboards and making banana bread.

Emotions were running high. Watching the infection rate and daily death toll rise, it was enough to push anyone to panic eat. Four months had passed when Boris announced the easing of the restrictions. Great! We get to see friends and family we hadn't seen in months. The excitement rose as plans were being made. Where will we go? Who will we see first? What will I wear? Oh! Four months of mindless eating turned out to be all fun and games until the jeans didn't zip up.

I'm in the business of helping and supporting others who are trying to lose weight. My business boomed overnight. Friends and locals now ready to get back to how they looked and felt before the lockdown descended upon us. Summer was here and we wanted to look our best to see everyone. My clientele doubled overnight.

Luckily I had maintained on the diet plan throughout the whole lockdown and lost up to seven stones. At the time the diet felt like it was the only thing I had control of for myself.

Fiona is a One2One Diet Consultant based in Ascot, Berkshire. She supports her clients with virtual consulting and delivering nutritional products to front doors. She considered gastric band or gastric sleeve surgery but The Plan worked.

Room 138 by Pat Abercromby

The big knickers were essential after the hip replacement. My leg swelled up to the size of a small (who am I kidding, a big) tree trunk. I 'convalesced' in a nursing home for a week in Room 138. The huge pants all displayed R138 in black felt tip pen on their labels in case they ended up adorning 137 other residents' behinds. I couldn't wait to get back into my high cut briefs and skinny jeans (image is everything isn't it?) The B.J. knickers as I called them, were pushed to the back of my underwear drawer to languish for all eternity. That was six years ago.

Then along came lockdown. No going out, living alone, boredom slips under the radar. The skinny jeans hang forlornly in the wardrobe. Might as well have another coffee break. The sun shines, the garden beckons, the cotton cut-offs with the elasticated waist are just the job. Thirsty work gardening, lots of tea breaks to stay hydrated with a ginger snap to dip. I rummage in the back of the drawer. Sighing, I pull on my Room 138 knickers and put the kettle on.

Pat is Scottish by birth but has lived in many overseas' locations, enjoyed several career pathways leading eventually to writing and publishing her first novel 'Just One Life' in her early 70s.

Weighing It All Up by Flip Webster

Lost – six friends and family – funerals unattended. Holidays, time with friends and family – some, forever. Swimming, Pilates, swing-dance. My work and joy – acting – an industry closed down. Income – gone. Meetings, auditions, events. Nearly lost my mind with building noise from the adjoining house when for months only allowed to leave the house one hour a day. Air and road traffic.

Gained – quiet. The birds reclaim the skies. Rainbows: some of the brightest I have ever seen. The air, fresher, sweeter. Tai Chi with my partner, script-readings on Zoom, walks, neighbourhood drinks on the street. No sudden deadlines and dashes into London. Time and space to address a mountain of things accumulated in my house over decades. Sifting through my life. So much paper! Equity activism, teaching materials, scripts, clippings, letters, cards, and props and costumes. Used and little-used things have been recycled and I have earned some money. Bags of stuff wait for the charity shops to reopen. Family history/memoir. Trawling through old memories as I sort stored things; the writing down of experiences; related feelings and thoughts have been a re-discovery.

In my late 60s I review my life, allow regrets, missed opportunities – the losses – and the great experiences – the gains – to be sifted, examined, along with my things: what takes me forward, what comforts my present and what I leave behind. Time for reflection allows me to decide how to spend my remaining years and how to end my story.

Flip is an actress and writer who has taken her shows to the Edinburgh Fringe, appeared in numerous plays, TV dramas and comedies, radio and films. She was trained at the Royal Central School of Speech and Drama. Originally from Devon she now lives in Kingston upon Thames.

Spending Time by Julie Goodman

I've often struggled with what I consider to be the currency of time. Spending it on the necessities of life is easy: work, daily chores, taking care of children. But it's the time that we call free, that I have trouble splurging. I find it easier to spend time on the practicalities of life, because these things are seen as selfless acts. In the past, using some of this precious currency on myself has found me in debt to the daily chores and I've had to pay it back.

In March 2020, the world offered me a loan. The conditions? Stay at home. Stop the school runs, stop washing those uniforms and packing lunches. I'd been given some interest-free time. I embraced every alarm-free morning, late breakfast and five minutes more before bed. I appreciated having my children at home, safe in one place. An hourglass, I'm always aware, is emptying by the day.

I read book after book. I learnt to crochet. And I put pen to paper. At the end of that time, some people will see a stack of novels, a couple of blankets and scribbles in a notebook. I see an investment in myself.

Julie lives in March, Cambridgeshire with her husband, three children and chocolate Labrador Jax. She is currently studying a creative writing course.

The Bad and the Good by Andrew Austen

No pubs, no clubs, no restaurants, no wandering abroad.
The risk we'll get bored.
No visits to ageing aunts. I'm an old boy now just thought I'd mention:
fully retired and on a pension.
But now I really want to go to work: stuck behind these four old walls.
Oh how I wish that duty calls.
This time I promise I won't shirk. No live sport.
No goals, tries or out caught.
I slouch eating cookies. My belly is growing.
Over my belt it is showing.
No racing so no bookies. The stats made bad reading.
Despair it was breeding.
But soon it will be in the past.
            AND
There were good things in this situation.
It's brought out the best in this island nation.
The NHS efforts have been just heroic:
brave, unselfish, unstinting and stoic.
There's now so much time for our DIY.
A second coat, too, once the first one is dry.
Learning so much as I hammer and screw.
Ignoring instructions and a bit of blood too.
Old friends have popped up on my screen.
Some I have known since my teens.
It's so good to see they look older than me
All in all it's not been ALL bad as happy was outweighed by sad.

Andrew spent over 40 years working for the Probation Service. He is from south London and, contrary to Samuel Johnson, wasn't tired of life when he moved to the country two years ago. He now has a new lease of life in rural Shropshire.

Growing On by Linda Ralph

So what has happened during the last six months? I've hardly seen the children, the grandchildren, my sister, family and friends. Oh, how I've missed those smiles, hugs and cuddles. The son's wedding has been delayed for a year. My outfit is on hold. Our summer in France didn't happen – no cherries, no hot tub, no pineau, no walnuts, no haute cuisine. I've missed the house parties there with family and friends; those balmy summer evenings sipping wine and exploring the stars with Sky View. The diet has collapsed. The winter cruise has been cancelled.

But my hair has grown and grown. I now have highly developed skills in shopping online. I've learnt the art of 'click and collect' for food shopping and promise myself never to push another huge trolley around a massive supermarket. I have found I can make a fair stab at doing 1000 piece jigsaws, and we've invested in a Scrabble board. My husband is now an ace baker of bread, an excellent curry maker and he has even started to organize his research on his family trees.

We do things together – and that ain't so bad! Together, we'll get through this.

Linda is a retired deputy head and a keen genealogist whose fifth limb is her laptop. She lives in Bexhill-on-Sea, Sussex.

Just the Season by Ian Gascoigne

'Two metres; please ensure you stay two metres apart at all times,' said the security.

Standing three metres from his guard, director Roland wondered if he'd missed the national switch from imperial to metric. He knew 'just over six feet and six inches' didn't have the same ring. Could they instead have stipulated seven feet, rounding up: the height of a giant? Once inside the museum, Roland knew distancing rules were not easy. People moved at different speeds. Gathering round a popular painting was normal. No one follows a precise route around exhibits, ignoring an interesting side room. It's not a route march. He estimated there were at least 50 people in the main gallery, probably 20 too many. No point in opening if you don't cover costs. From the doorway he heard the first sneeze in the reverential silence. A murmur and a gasp followed. People's hurried movements almost masked the second one. Roland wasn't close enough for identification, but the shoving was unmistakeable. He asked for calm.

A man in a blue gilet was gesticulating to the dispersing group. 'Relax. It's hay fever. I suffer every June.'

'Well, suffer alone,' a lady said, pointing her catalogue. 'Outside.'

Ian is a lawyer based in Buckinghamshire and new as a writer.

Cashing In by Elaine Mulvaney

Yesterday, in search of a little excitement, I walked to my local Co-Op for some absolute essentials: a child's comic, glittery sprinkles to put on a cake. Ahead at the checkout, an old lady. It was obviously the first time she'd been out for, oooh, she didn't know how long. That would explain why she wasn't aware of the proper etiquette now. Chatting. Laboriously extracting the last bit of money from her battered old purse. Revelling in her freedom. Get a move on!

And the youth on the till was delighted to see her again after all this time, hoping she'd stay safe, although the last bit had to be repeated a few times as she couldn't quite hear. Will this ever end? I was silent but visceral. I needed to get on. (Not strictly true.)

She turned to go, misstepped, dropped a few coins and, when, automatically, I bent down too, my head bumped hers and my hand touched her hand. I sprang back.

It was the first time I had touched another human being for almost a year.

Elaine won Creative Ink's 'Dear John, Dear Anyone …' monologue competition and her winning piece 'Dear Jane' was filmed along with eleven other finalists.

Shopping Around by Margaret Gardner

I never thought a trip to a supermarket would be a wonderful treat, but as I drove the seventeen miles down to Asda this week I felt as if a whole new world was opening up before me. And as if that wasn't enough, as I walked round the superstore I was assailed by a choice of items such as I hadn't seen since lockdown in March and felt almost overwhelmed. The thought that this could become a regular pastime once the pandemic is over seems almost inconceivable, but it gives me hope for a brighter shopping future, an escape from the confines of my local stores with their basic and restricted food choices, their narrow aisles and higher prices.

I have surprised myself with how much I have missed such shopping trips. Deprived of the opportunity to buy exotic ingredients my cooking has reverted to more basic meals, and I find myself salivating at the mere possibility of returning to a more varied cuisine. At the moment we still do not venture far from home, but Asda is there, beckoning to me, and all it will take is time …

Margaret is a retired teacher and runs a creative writing group for Petersfield U3A, Hampshire.

The Vicious Cycle by Libby Evans

As Cyril finished his egg he visualized the headlines: *Cyril the Cyclist Saves Our Souls.* Everyone knew that because of the deadly virus all shops should be shut except for essential ones: foodies, pharmacies and cycle accessories. But the Garden Centre was open!

Cyril was going on a mission, he would do his bit, he would be one of those people eligible to shop early at Waitrose, and the world will be a safer place. He checked his Lycra for aerodynamic performance, pumped his tyres up and set off with wings on his shoulders and fire in his saddle.

The approach to the Garden Centre was a steep 20 miles per hour hill which Cyril coasted at 30 miles per hour. Quite legal as speed was the essence of his mercy mission. He swept into the car park and positioned himself across the entrance and screamed. 'They're killing our children, they're killing our doctors! They only want our money! Go home everyone! Save the world!'

He aimed an open-mouthed cough at the manager who tried to explain that their food hall was open ... Cyril peddled off congratulating himself, aware that something must be done about his saddle.

Perhaps the cycle shop would be open?

Libby went to Hull Art College in the 1950s. Then she came south to work at Goya cosmetic firm as a designer. When she married, business was one green house and a shed. Eventually her husband had five garden centres but now there are just two. She has done all aspects of art including adverts and posters for the business.

What's Missing? by Sarah Abercromby Mann

Shops have been closed, no cars to drive.
What's the point of swimming pools
if there is no one to dive?
Most places have no money to survive
but somehow fish and chips still seem alive.
No people to roam the deserted streets.
Lockdown strikes when for once we have heat.
Incomes lost, friendships destroyed,
people get fired instead of employed.
None truly knows what caused this virus.
Do not believe gossip because panic means liars.
Only emergencies call for healthcare
because being in hospital is rare.
Essential workers are doing their best.
We all clap at eight to show we're impressed.
Playing games to distract us from reality.
Everyone knows Covid robs your vitality.
Get masks they say, they will save us all,
but what use is that, there's none available!
We're all going through this just the same
though we might be turning clinically insane.
Everyone knew it would be hard no doubt.
I'm finding it tough and I never go out.
I definitely thought it'd be easier than this.
But why am I sad if there's no one to miss?

*Sarah is ten years old and is from Beaconsfield,
Buckinghamshire.*

Bin Day by Anita Evans

What do we do from day to day?
To while the time away a whole heap of arbitrary things.
Like mending tools with broken springs.
Whilst out walking we learn to sidestep out of the way
of other strollers to try to keep this virus at bay.
In these uncertain times
face creams will not hide the worry lines
but a friendly wave
really lifts up your spirits to make you brave
and ready to face yet another quiet day.
We look forward to bin day
and savour the noise
but it is not the same as hearing children play on their toys.
It is so eerily quiet especially when you live by yourself
pretending to be busy re-arranging shelf by shelf!
The NHS staff need all our wholehearted support
and those caring for the vulnerable and overwrought.
This virus has caught us unawares
leaving innumerable bereft.
It has caused us all to feel very frightened and stressed
but our Queen gave us a compassionate speech
proudly reminding us of our predecessors
who stepped into the breach.
Meanwhile we will endeavour to keep in touch
with those we dearly love and cherish but cannot hug.
But remember that a kindly acknowledging shrug
can mean so very much.

Anita walked into Jan's class one day but found the deadlines far too scary. She went away but she was taught to be less wary.

Coffee Froth by Victoria Gentle

After all this is over
I will sit in a coffee shop
warm through glass,
savouring the hum of everyday conversation.
Coffee machine will grind:
sweet music to my ears.
Frothy swirls chat and dance.
Plates clatter offstage.
Someone laughs.
Lips licking in sugary anticipation,
eyes closed
I will lean back
and drink in heaven.
Ordinary,
hum-drum,
pulsing,
alive.
Heaven.

In a coffee shop.

Victoria is a mum of two and a drama teacher from Hertfordshire, who also has a passion for the great outdoors and storytelling in all its forms. In her spare time she likes to combine her poetry, meditations and art inspired by nature and family life on Instagram at: www.instagram.com/gentlepoetry

Summer of Love Scrubs by Kate Collet-Fenson

There is a group sixty-five people – most I met over WhatsApp or socially distanced on the doorstep. We became 'something' after a few random appeals on our community Covid WhatsApp group and the Aston Hearing newsletter. We gathered momentum as our messages and word of our mission spread – until we became the Loosley Row and Friends Sewing Group.

Sixty of us making PPE for the frontline. As part of the national Love for Scrubs movement my role, as founder of our group, was fundraising, co-ordinating, distributing, packing, posting, delivering, receiving and supporting this super-talented group of wonderful women. Their tireless stitching and sewing produced over the period of the first hot summer lockdown, thousands of wash bags, headbands, scrub caps. Two hundred and forty pairs of scrubs were wonderfully sewn with love and sent out to hospitals, GPs, care homes, ambulance crews, Covid hubs locally and beyond.

I met most of the group but they didn't meet each other. When this is all over we made a promise to ourselves to have a street party in Loosley Row to finally meet and celebrate our Summer of Love. Scrubs stitching and WhatsApp friendships were forged at a social distance and our collective memories will certainly outlive the garments we made. But it met a most urgent need in the most quirky, beautiful way that will stay with us all forever.

Kate is the Loosley Row Founder and Co-ordinator of The Loosley Row & Friends Sewing Group. She is also owner of Aston Hearing in Buckinghamshire.

Darning by Tina Jackson

We are stitching together holes:
the rent in our fabric.
We zoom across time zones, hands busy
with needles and thread, silks and woollens,
poisoned gardens and a pilgrim's progress.
A whole alphabet of imaginary beings
and holey socks and jumpers that have seen better days.
We unravel not just floss and fabric but
old friends' stories of then and how and when and where
and who and what and why.
We each sit in our webs spinning yarns.
Passing time as people have done through time:
makers, crafters, weavers, menders,
all the accidental seamsters and seamstresses
who mend socks, patch cloth,
repair the tiny tears that turned to years,
tend to the warp and weft of past and present.
We are
sew sew.
Happy to patch things together.
We sew crows, stitch frogs, unfrog what goes wrong
as we mend our ways,
piecing together scraps more precious for history.
Yet not worn out.
We'll make sure it holds together.
Strong threads stand the test of time.

Tina is a UK writer and journalist and Assistant Editor at 'Writing Magazine'. Her debut novel 'The Beloved Children' was published in 2020 by Fahrenheit Press and she's the author of a collection of short stories and a book on suffrage history.

Lost Weddings by Elizabeth Bessant

I am involved in the couture design process – whether a wedding dress, mother-of-bride outfit or accessories – from initial consultation to collection. And there has certainly been a lot of lost weddings this past year. Some of my brides whose dresses I started pre-lockdown have had their weddings cancelled three times and are now hoping to go ahead after June 2021. Two gave up and opted for small weddings and are going to have a big party later in the year.

I felt only a bride could express the real truth about it and contacted Crystal whose wedding should have gone ahead in April 2020 for her thoughts: 'It was heart breaking for me, it was the most terrible feeling ever. I had anxiety attacks and couldn't sleep for three months. The sad part was that I wanted it so badly, the dream wedding I had planned and couldn't have. There was nothing anyone could say or do to help and after three cancellations I opted for a small wedding and I've never been happier'. Lockdown bride Crystal Rose.

Elizabeth has a loyal following of celebrity and society clients. Outfits are made in her London studio by her team of skilled crafts people. www.elizabethbessant.co.uk

Another Bride ... by Angela Andrews

April 5th was in lockdown,
the wedding postponed,
the reception quickly cancelled,
one hundred and fifty guests duly phoned.

The misery, the sadness
the cost of it all;
the planning ,the shopping
the details so small.

Five months crawled by,
restrictions constantly changed;
a quick decision was made
a September date arranged.

You applied your own makeup,
your best friend did your hair;
we cut our own flowers
and I drove you there

in my old car with its memories
as we travelled to new;
that time will ever be precious,
Yellow MG, me and you.

We strode down the aisle
tearfully holding hands;
thirty socially spaced guests
and a few zoomed from other lands.

I've never seen you so radiant,
smiling with utter delight;
holding hands with your new husband,
beautiful, everything so right.

When this is all over
will we need the 'big do'
the dancing, the folk band,
the expensive venue ?

Angela is a wife, mother, aspiring poet, and now resides in Great Missenden, Buckinghamshire. As Angela Dennison she sold advertising space for 'Rhyme & Reason' during the years around the millennium.

Where Will We Go? by Andrea Wotherspoon

We write a list of places to go when this is all over. I thought we'd choose locations far from our tiny town on the north coast of Scotland: Glasgow, London, New York, Japan, Morocco, Iceland. But the places we long for aren't distant and new to us, but nearby and familiar.

Dunbeath Strath, with the scent of wild garlic and the coconut smell of gorse, the *tea-cher* call of a great tit. We'll explore the Iron Age broch and the ruined coaching inn.

Duncansby Head, where fluffy fulmar chicks and jaunty puffins perch on guano-covered ledges. Clumps of red campion, dirty sheep's wool caught on barbed wire. We'll stop at Puffin Croft on the way, feed carrots to the goats and buy flapjacks to eat in the car.

Dunnet Beach on a hazy day, miles of pale sand and sloping dunes. We'll collect razor shells and make a sandcastle.

Red wine, tapas and laughter with friends at Capilla; post-Parkrun breakfast at Y-Not bar; a Sunday evening barbeque with family. A drive to Scrabster, where we'll watch the Orkney ferry leave and the fishing boats unload their catch.

These are the places we'll go when this is all over.

Andrea is based in the far north of Scotland. She writes fiction inspired by birds, the sea and local legends.

Fata Morgana Mirage by Anthony Lyons

We arrived back in the UK two days before lockdown in March 2020. We had been crossing the Pacific: 40 days of island hopping in our own bubble. We really couldn't believe what was happening or indeed how long it would go on for. Travelling is our passion and over the last twelve months of this pandemic we have seen so many of our adventures fall foul to the cancellation wave which is still lapping around our feet keeping us firmly rooted in the UK.

The feeling of house arrest still remains with us and the hope of parole is now on the horizon but is it a Fata Morgana mirage? Our suitcases will need dusting down but our passports stand ready to be once again presented to an immigration officer who looks like he has just sucked on a lemon.

We will never again complain of waiting for flights at the airport, not having a hotel room available when we check in.

The joys of travel.

Anthony is from Ascot, Berkshire.

A Dreaming Triolet of Lisboa by Jeni Scott

Vasco da Gama left from there.
Lisbon's ancient steps lead down
to spumy ocean. Cracked balconies

rise and billow on Alfama hills.
Beggars hover in Figueras Square.
Vasco da Gama left from there.

Crumbling edifice, daubed in paint.
Hawkers cry, spit, sell their wares.
Smokey pillars left of the past.
Vasco da Gama left from there.

Jeni left her native Scotland in 1970 to work overseas with her new husband. After numerous moves and countries, they arrived in Beaconsfield, Buckinghamshire. There she became involved with 'Rhyme & Reason' magazine whilst teaching creative writing in Adult Education, eventually becoming an editor (2004-2006). She writes: 'This was a satisfying and very happy time'.

No Tennis at the End of June by Lois Hambleton

Blossom at each window but no tennis at the end of June. No dazzling whites, no breathless rallies.

When I heard the gunshot, meant for the gentle pheasant in the uncut field, I found the bullet in the ground and curled my fingers tight around its weight. Warm from the mechanism, that mortal chamber, reminding me of fissions, separating, splitting up. But then of fusion, thrust aligning with the April sun and warm, just like the blood, the flesh the missile would have torn, if just an atom further …

The peaceful pheasant, gentle at my door takes cake from out of my sparrow hand and stands bewildered of that lethal force, devoid of atoms yet it runs its course. One shot, it's spent, unlike the little viral sprite that dances, joyous, atom bright. Don't breathe the air…

Deprived of anatomic bind, of sons and daughters that have left the nest, I seek to catch their colours, keep their blood, their flesh, their feathers. Perhaps the pheasant fills my void but here's the main and only thing – no tennis at the end of June …

Lois is a retired Adult Education lecturer from Birmingham, now living in Shropshire.

My Uncle's War Diary by Marion Mackett

On the 9th January 1940 George Mackett enlisted into the Royal Regiment of Artillery. His battery trained and defended England before being posted overseas. The six years he spent abroad he recorded, as brief notes, places visited and his feelings.

'25th December 1941. Christmas Day, somewhere in mid-Atlantic, shelled, German raider, convoy split up.

14th March l941. First mail from England.

3rd February 1942. Left Ack site at Tobruck, for rest (we hope).

22nd June l942. Tobruck fell to the Germans … situation does not look good.

14th January 1943. Near Alexandria, small tents, hate it, very cold and damp.

6th May 1943. Ten miles along Tripoli road … sea is very nice for bathing.

24th September 1943. Arrived in Taranto, Italy…'tis grand to be in green country.

6th June 1944. Gosh I'm homesick. At dawn allied troops landed in France, what news at last.

5th August 1945. After nearly six years peace has come. Japan surrendered.

26th January l946. Released – happiest day of my life.'

This book of memories just touches on the tenacity and courage of our brave soldiers, one of whom I am proud to be related to. Having read the war diary of my uncle I realized he survived six years of the turbulent, emotional pandemic of World War Two. His words more powerful than guns, evoking the devastation of the time but maintaining his belief in a better future.

Marion is from Dorset and has published 'Jasper's Clever Plan' with Fuzzypig Books.

Haiku by Hugh Hodge

Noise annoys old songs
of longing, of memory,
of times before this.

Remembering May 1945 by Robert Shooter

Wilf's pandemic anxiety was so debilitating he couldn't do what he wanted to. It was five years since his wife died and he'd got used to being on his own. He looked at his piano, crying out for him to play. He looked at his tablet. There were people he could chat with. Or stuff he could write. He went out into his garden looking at the weeds that needed picking, even cheeky dandelions smiling at him from the lawn. 'Out damn spot,' he shouted.

Carl shouted from the garden next door. 'Are you murdering something or someone?'

'Dandelions,' Wilf said, pointing.

Carl nodded, understanding.

Wilf suddenly remembered a huge crater caused by a doodle bomb landing in their garden. A few feet north and the house would have gone with him, his sister and Mum. Dad returned home sometime in 1945 and filled it in. Wilf realized this perishing Covid-19 virus, which could kill and nobody could do anything to protect until a vaccine, was invented was freezing him. He went in to do stuff.

July 2020

Robert was a social worker in London, Wales and Lancashire and has worked as a hospital chaplain in Blackpool, Lancashire. He has now retired to East Yorkshire.

Blitz Spirit Again by Philip Burton

On the first night, when the docks were hit
and orange glow seemed to chew the far end
off the Fulham Palace Road, he sat quiet for a bit
then sharpened his spade in the old back shed.

He loved his quiet life, on Averill Street
but Grandad stopped his job with the Gas Board.
Not digging for victory, he said. It's about retreat.
Beneath the rhubarb bed, into marl and chalk

he hewed a massive crypt, and all the neighbours
would spend each night and sleep easy there.
When the war was done, his mighty labours
scarcely made a scratch on history, that I'm aware.

So, when this pandemic is tamed, let's not forget
the essential folk, but raise them on our shoulders:
they who sweated their days, had no relief, and yet
they soldiered on. They should be Dames and Sirs.

Philip is a family man, living in Bacup, a former Lancashire head teacher, and has also been as Pip the Poet, a poetry practitioner for children. His poetry publications include 'The Raven's Diary' (published 1998), 'Couples'/Clitheroe Books Press 2008, 'His Usual Theft'/Indigo Dreams Press 2017 and 'Gaia Warnings'/Palewell Press 2021.

Street Party by Laila Murphy

My last street party was when Charles and Diana got married. I was a toddler, the same age as my son, and I don't remember any of it.

I imagine there'll be tables with mismatching chairs, and a mixture of home-baked goods with shop-bought sausage rolls. Kids running wild. Beer and wine. Laughter continuing into the night, long after those with families have retired, sun-soaked and worn out.

I mentioned the idea casually, but others seized it hungrily; it was something we could look forward to. The WhatsApp group started with a note and mobile number, pushed through every letterbox, during a time of unease. Practically every household responded. For months, our phones have pinged with requests for help with shopping, lockdown memes, swaps for rakes and travel sickness tablets, fence paint and baby seats. We started a book club. I left bread on someone's doorstep. She brought me homemade scones. Every Thursday, we emerged to clap for the NHS and wave at each other, chatting with those nearest.

One day, we'll bring those tables and mismatched chairs into the road, cover them with tablecloths, lay them with food. Our kids will run wild. We'll meet properly, at last.

Laila is from Liverpool. She is the librarian at a lively all-girls secondary school. When she is not recommending books, teaching, or hosting events, she is raising her little son Hugo with her partner Conor. She writes short stories and enters them into competitions every chance she gets! Laila was one of the twelve finalist scriptwriters in Creative Ink's film 'Dear John, Dear Anyone …' in 2012.

Happy Birthday, Waterside Theatre, Aylesbury
by Lesley Christofi

Ten years since her journey began
bringing culture and arts to the town.
But events since March intervened
and forced us to bring her curtain down.

Standing majestically in the heart of the town
this beautiful building opened in 2010.
Its productions and staff and her crews
have been entertaining audiences since then.

We should be celebrating ten years of shows,
ten years since she opened her doors.
Instead she stands empty and dark
waiting to light up our lives once more.

Resilience and endurance will overcome,
she is waiting for us sturdy and strong.
She'll be there waiting for us all to return,
so be assured that the shows WILL go on.

Lesley is a doting grandma and 'resting' stage door keeper from Hertfordshire. Her son is a former Creative Ink stage manager who kept all the bits together for us. She loves family history, theatre and music.

Playing Our Part by Pat Brewin

Rehearsing outside in the garden. We could try a pantomime kiss, standing six feet apart, with a sound effect. Mmm, might distract from the sinister nature of the play I thought, but top marks for creativity. The rain began to fall, my script damp and crumpled. 'Is she dead?' My cue, missed. What will the neighbours think? Will they report us for breaking the rules, one too many people staring at the weeds, waiting for the clouds to pass, or for being a suspected murderer? What is the point? We can't perform it anywhere soon. Perhaps we could do it outside, socially distanced, in November. What, to an audience of Eskimos and the most loyal of partners?

November came and went, as did the outside rehearsals, Zoom too with no movement or set. A village hall awaits and no, she isn't dead.

Pat was originally from Croydon, Surrey – now living in Chester. Although she never realized her ambition as a seven-year-old to be a professional comedy actor she has provided a few laughs, often unintentionally, in am-dram societies such as Guilden Sutton Players, TipTop productions, Company55 and Centrestage, Mold.

Dreaming of the Fringe by Phillip Sheahan

William sat bolt upright and mopped the sweat from his fevered brow. His fingers fumbled for the iPhone. He pressed the 'record' app. His vision for *A Midsummer Night's Dream* emerged through the corona fog. Breathless he whispered, 'The four lovers ... randy rabbits each socially distanced by four cubits ... Oberon and Titania ... a pair of macaws, bickering through surgical masks. The mechanicals? ... Pyramus, a capitalist unicorn, Thisbe, a doe-eyed proletarian fawn, share their love of shopping through the chink in a wall of toilet rolls. The Lion? The claw of state controlling and devouring transgressors! Puck? ... No! Mischievous 'Wuhan': the pandemic spirit, who's put a girdle around the earth.'

A smile blossomed on William's face. He was as happy as Titania when she loved an ass. This will be the finest production that The Covid-19 Players ever took to Edinburgh!

'The Spectator' magazine invited submissions for a competition on a 'Love in the Time of Covid-19' theme: 150 words of magical realism. Phillip's efforts produced a published 'commended' accolade, which this native Australian of long British residency will remember as an isolation highlight to add to his collection of other sparks of joy for stories, plays, poems and speeches. Phillip was one of the twelve scriptwriting finalists in Creative Ink's film 'Dear John, Dear Anyone ...' 2012.

Browsing Suspension by Rosemary Benham

Well – here we all are, looking at our weekly calendar rather that our yearly one. I am still working at my library and although browsing has been suspended, we 'serve' at the door, and can still chat, with a mask and two metres between us. My customers can request books generally, or reserve titles which go on to a trolley at the door, and they just take them. I deliver audio books to a couple of my registered blind customers who live near my library. We all try to look after our vulnerable customers as well as the fighting fit ones.

Generally it's my older customers who are always looking on the bright side, and checking to see how I am. It's so uplifting. They're a stoic lot. I hadn't heard from one of my elderly couples for a while, so called them for a chat. They were worried about coming to pick up their books in case they were stopped by the police and fined. The husband did pop in and said his wife had been a bit down that day, and my call had lifted her spirits.

Small things mean a lot to all of us, don't they?

Rosemary spent her formative years in Croydon, Surrey and escaped to Crowborough, East Sussex in the 1980s. She worked primarily in architecture but in the last eleven years has been running the lovely Wadhurst Library.

The Lock Road Little Free Library
by Diarmaid Fitzpatrick

Just before the doors closed last year for the first lockdown, I phoned my friend James to ask him if he would help me with a project. James has a wonderfully equipped workroom and I called him because I had an idea to build a replica of a 'Little Free Library' my son-in-law Phillip had installed outside his house in Melbourne.

When all this is over and Covid-19 has been overcome I will remember the generosity of James and his wife Claire when they welcomed me to stay in their home, while James and I worked on the project. James, with the skill and patience of a master craftsman guided me in the creation of what was to become 'The Lock Road Little Free Library'. Since its opening in July 2020, and all through the pandemic it has seen a steady flow of avid readers bringing and borrowing books of all genres, spy novels, bodice rippers, books on Health and Wellbeing, gardening and nutrition. And I will also remember the smiles on people's faces when they found a favourite book to take home and read.

Diarmaid is 73 and lives in Marlow, Buckinghamshire. In 1987 after 35 years working in the hotel industry in Dublin, London, Frankfurt, Munich, Dusseldorf, Edinburgh and the Sultanate of Oman, he settled down with his family to live in Marlow. He was involved in the initial setting up of Transition Town Marlow, and presented the 'Bizz Buzz' programme on Marlow FM for five years. Now semi-retired he continues to work as a certified shadow work group facilitator and coach offering one to one coaching and online webinars.

Isolation Advice from Jane Austen
by Phillip Sheahan

It is a truth universally acknowledged, that a single man in possession of a large hamper, must be in want of sexual congress. The knock upon your door, the polite retreat of three yards, the gesture to the groceries at your feet are all but the performance of a peacock. He may enquire with mock concern whether you are 'well'. Nothing is more deceitful. It is but a ploy to solicit a statement indicating your need for close companionship. Be firm but polite in your reply. Inform the gentleman that you have a cat and have been agreeably self-isolating with an excellent book. Your mind has been stimulated and your appetite for other excitements satisfied by two squares of fudge at four o'clock. If the gentleman wishes to call again ask the name of his grocer. Should the words 'food bank' be uttered … need I say more?

Isolation Advice from George Orwell
by Phillip Sheahan

Self-isolation need not be a dystopian nightmare. Locked down with only your inner demons to wrestle with provides both mental agility and physical exercise. When researching *Animal Farm* I isolated with Farmer Jones for three weeks in his outside privy with but a single roll of lavatory paper between us. Sheets were allocated by games of rock, paper, scissors. I, being intellectually superior, won most games. Poor Jones managed on just three sheets of paper for the entire duration. It was only then that I truly understood the suffering of dumb animals. A repeat of my isolation experiment in room 101 was less successful. I was unable to acquire a rat and tried to make do with a hamster. I feel in love with the hamster and it loathed me: an emotional disaster for us both. Keep a diary. Isolation provides valuable expletives for 'new speak'. 'Love in the time of Covid-19.'

A Year for the Books by Kirsty Jackson
CEO and Co-Owner of Cranthorpe Millner Publishers

This past year has been strange, to say the least. One for the books, both figuratively and literally. Our industry has faced some real hardships, like so many others, and has had to adjust to countless rather unusual events but it has done so admirably and come up fighting! This year has introduced complications that we have never had to face before and we're humbled by everyone's continued support and our authors' relentless, positive attitudes.

There has been some positivity to come out of all this. Because, if anything, this past year has taught us that people will never stop reading. And many people found that working from home provided them with the opportunity to finally get that book finished that they've been trying to write for years. Books – be they paperback or eBooks – will always hold an important place in people's hearts and in the world as a whole. Where would we be without them? It fills me with joy every day that I get to be a part of and contribute to this industry.

Kirsty is from Cambridge and her publishing company is based there. www.cranthorpemillner.com

Corona Confinement in Kent by Isabel MacLeod

It has been a time for reflection. Each day during lockdown, I go out for an hour's walk. The weather has been glorious and I am lucky to live in a rural spot surrounded by beautiful countryside: that has made this awful situation more tolerable. The woods and fields are my playground.

I have watched the beauty of the season developing. Bluebells and primroses replaced daffodils, tiny plants have become fields of flowering oilseed rape. Some days, when the light is just right, I am Elizabeth Bennet tripping joyfully along a grassy path to Netherfield: albeit a rather older 66-year-old version. Perhaps I could be Charles Dickens striding round the Kent countryside...

I have seen nesting skylarks, rising into the air singing, whilst protecting their nest from marauding starlings. I am tempted to quote Shelley, but don't disturb the beauty of the moment. Some things I have long known. Family is paramount: their safety, good health and happiness. I have missed my grandchildren enormously, but they are all right, nothing else is so important.

What have I learned? Former certainties have been swept away and we need to learn to live differently.

Summer 2020

Isabel grew up in suburban Croydon, Surrey and has lived, worked and enjoyed family life in North Kent for over 40 years, where she also pursues a variety of interests amongst which she researched and wrote two books about the history of a school: Selhurst Grammar School for Girls.

A Midsummer Dream by Sarah-Jane Reeve

I dreamt I was walking but suddenly, I felt dread. What about home? Had I left the front door open? A restless breeze blew leaves towards me and among them I saw paper masks. I retraced my steps along the track. The front door was wide open, and written on it were my passwords for all to see.

`Hello,' I called, but there was only silence.

I climbed stairs carpeted in fading equations and headlines: R is up to twenty. My family was gone. The floors were littered with banknotes and air tickets. The cat looked up from her quarantine on the bookcase; her eyes were moonbeams and the books were unread. She meowed and the sound was the rustle of a million leaves. She climbed into my arms and realizing there were no goodbyes we ran to the waiting trees.

Deep in the wood I knew it was all over. Breathing freely, soothed by birdsong. At the oak tree I pulled back the blanket of moss. I lay down in the earth like a seed and the falling leaves covered me. The trees sighed.

'Stay,' they said. `You can be rooted and still touch the sky.'

Sarah-Jane worked in publishing for many years and now lives in Berkshire with her husband and two daughters.

The Fat Lady Sings by Carrie Williams

Dad,

We saw one another less and talked more on the phone. We shared information gathered from Sky News, following the disease marching through Europe and then beyond. I did your shopping and dropped it off on your doorstep. You paid me by leaving £20 notes wet from bacterial spray on the car dashboard. You cut the lawn and hedges and I got you a new iPad which I slid into the hallway. I gave you lessons on Zoom and you left some features until we could sit down together again.

You suddenly became fatigued and put it down to not having had your B12 injection due to Covid restrictions. I took you for blood tests and X-rays in ghostly corridors and empty hospitals and further tests were arranged. You decided to get admitted to hospital to find out what was going on. We knew it meant you being on your own and that I couldn't see you. Paramedics arrived and whisked you off to the red zone of A & E as your blood pressure was dangerously low. I waved goodbye reassuring you from the pavement and bent over double as the ambulance drove away.

The next day you phoned and said, 'Not good news. I knew you'd be upset. I'll be 90 next year. I could have died from Covid.' You had worked so hard not to.

The doctor told me, 'He doesn't seem to accept the situation that there's nothing can be done'.

I told the faceless voice, 'My dad always believes something can be done. For my father, it will never be over 'till the fat lady sings'.

We got you home. Then three weeks of masks, aprons, catheters, injections, carers, doctors alongside day-to-day

Covid restrictions. On 28th July I asked, 'Where's the pain, Dad?'

'All over,' you replied.

Those were your last words. I'd been saying it for weeks. 'It won't be over 'till the fat lady sings.'

For Roy Humphries. (1st August 1931-29th July 2020)

Carrie is from Cardiff, South Wales and spent many years in the professional theatre as an actress and a singer before having a career as a social worker. She performed in Creative Ink's film, 'Dear John, Dear Anyone …'

Haiku by Hugh Hodge

Only ghosts remain
now the unbottled spirits
flee poem and song.

Presentiment by Patricia Sentinella

August is baleful,
full of thunder bugs and omens
breathing on my skin.

Wrapped in newsprint
I nurse the cold in my head.
Only the sound of the rain
seeps through.

Lulled by library books
and linctus, I wait,

remembering past summers,
their small bereavements,
smells of burning,
London streets hot
and empty as these fields.

Then the shadow-fall
as the month turns,
as the page turns
to the dark calendar
hooked in my heart.

First published in Patricia's collection 'Dear John, Dear Anyone ...'/Creative Ink Publishing.

Hope You Are Well by Lynne Potter

Not the shaky I'm fine to the question, 'How are you?'
Nor the long distance Zoom that stretches the gap to
breaking point.
Or the gulf between pretend hugs and air kisses.
Not one thousand piece jigsaw filling the time.
Nor voice on the telephone straining to sound cheerful.
Or the surprise of a tidy wardrobe and lined up shoes.
Not the boxes of books piled high in the garage for charity.
Nor the floral and plain masks hanging on hooks by the
door.
Or four walls threatening to crush your spirit. It's in …
Breathing fresh air, in day-to-day comforts, in happy
memories, making our lives while we can.

*Lynne is a member of the Hexham writing group,
Northumberland.*

Leashed by Martha Wells Bess

Can somebody tell me what's happening?
I'd really like to know
why my life has become so restricted.
'Cos it's causing a bit of woe.

Oh yes, we still go out walking,
but now, always on the lead.
Why can't I run like I used to?
It's a sorry state indeed.

And all of my neighbourhood, long-time pals
at a distance I have to pass.
No more racing round till you're dizzy.
No more gambolling on the grass.

I can't have fun with Buttons,
or run around with Rover.
So I dream of the day – not too far away?
When whatever it is will be over.

Martha was born in Aberdeen, Scotland where she trained as a general nurse, took maternity training in England. Went round the world in her twenties, starting at the Toronto General and working her way west from there. On her return home, she took the Health Visitor course, again in Aberdeen, where she has lived since.

A Dog's Life by Alexa James

You died on 6th August, while the first wave of Covid was lapping at the world's shores. Forty-nine people in the U.K had died, bringing the death toll to 46,413. It was before the statistical jiggery pokery began. It was before the heatwave, when the flocks crowded on to the Covid-on-Sea beaches.

You were not my dog. You belonged to our neighbour, but our house was your second home. After a shot of immune suppressive medication in April, I adhered to the shielding rule and I didn't see you or my neighbour for a few Covid-stealing weeks. The night before you died, I stroked you, with plastic gloves on my hands to protect myself and anyone else who stroked you.

Sometimes the after-life seems as hard to believe in as AstraZeneca pulling a vaccinated rabbit out of the hat. Perhaps it's safest to go with 'Pascal's Wager'.

If I take a bet on the afterlife for humans, I'm prepared to take a long a shot for an animal. That night I ask Jesus to allow the 49 people to enter into the light of His face. And I ask that a honey-coloured, loving dog might just play at His feet.

Tilly by Maureen Taylor

Tilly is limping.

'She's nine now,' you say. 'She's getting old, like me!'

In the lane outside your door, we sit every day, six feet apart, finding the crossword harder as the year of staying safe goes on. The vet, Sarah, passes by.

'Tilly's got a limp,' you say.

Sarah feels the dog's joints. 'It seems to be a bit of arthritis. How old is she now?'

'She's seven. She's getting old, like me!' You smile.

'I'll drop off a painkiller. No, don't worry. There isn't a charge. I've got supplies at home.'

You are relieved at not having to worry about getting Tilly to the surgery. Mostly, you are delighted at this special treatment. You go inside to get another drink and when you come out you say, 'Tilly's got a sore leg. She's ten now. She's getting old, like me! Sarah had a look and said it's arthritis. She's going to drop off a painkiller. She's got supplies at home. She won't take any money. Isn't that kind?'

'Yes,' I say. 'Very kind.'

My smile feigns warmth whilst my spirit shivers. You will never regain what you have lost this year, even when this is all over.

Maureen writes that she is fortunate to live in Northumberland where they have lots of open spaces on the doorstep which has been a great advantage during this period of restrictions.

Pamela's Pandemic by Pamela Mintner

This is the big pause.

One benefit is seeing my husband James 24/7. We cherish each other's company, would you believe? My son was 'let go' from his dog walking company. So together we have started his own dog walking business. My daughter put her Streatham studio on the market and moved into our family barn. She had acquired a partner, a puppy and now works from home. Her partner has lost his job, now works freelance and cannot get the same mortgage. It is hard for the young!

We oldies are forced to update our technology skills: for deliveries, family Zoom calls, WhatsApp and even Facebook. We watch more Netflix, BBC iPlayer, Sky... My property business has slowed and I have to help out several tenants. In the local community, I volunteer for phone support. Many are helping out ... it is uplifting! The British spirit is alive and well. The world has changed: more technology and working from home; more successes such as our vaccine discoveries and rollout!

Pamela is looking for a publisher for her book: 'Diary of a Desert Dream' about the transformation of the Emirates, where she worked in broadcasting.

Escape by Marie Day

When this time is all over
from lockdown I'll be free.
I'll saunter on the seafront
my face turned toward the sea.

We'll stroll the prom together,
ahead our famous pier.
We'll walk the planks and ride the train.
We'll touch without a fear.

The sea will shine and glisten
in the brightness of the sun.
We'll be in this place together
when isolation's done.

No more virtual travelling.
No more staying home.
Time to take the salty air.
To wander and to roam.

I promise I'll remember
the joy of being free.
To never take for granted
the chance to simply be.

So when this time is over
I hope you'll guarantee.
Remind me of my promise
facing out toward the sea.

Marie is a retired school teacher and lives in Southend-on-Sea, Essex.

The Lake by Susannah White

I long to sit beside a fishing lake,
and spend my time watching the ducks drift by.
No fears or doubts,
no piles of bills to pay,
no one to take offence
at what I do
or say.

My lake will sparkle
in the morning sun.
My only focus will be catching fish.
Fears and resentments will be lost
then gone.
Time by a fishing lake is all I wish.

Susannah writes English GCSE revision guides for 'York Notes' and she enjoys going fishing with her husband in her spare time. She lives in Cirencester, Gloucestershire near the Cotswold Water Park.

Sky and Soil by Kathryn Wharton

I will kiss a clean sky,
cherish the stoic bark
of ancient trees
and hug them.

I will not bemoan
the cost of life. I'll grow
herbs and vegetables,
I will be sustainable.

When this is over
I'll watch butterflies migrate
and the seasons return
to their natural place.

When this is over
I'll walk careful on earth,
or tend to spring
in the comfort of soil.

Kathryn is a poet from Baildon in West Yorkshire. Since completing her MA in Creative Writing at Leeds Trinity University, she has been working on a poetry collection. Poetry has been a means of sustaining herself through the present crisis.

The Worst Gardener by John Moore

Even the worst gardener in Britain can do it.

'Gojis grow in the Himalayas,' he boomed. 'They survive deep snow, heavy rain, drought and floods. They grow almost anywhere. If your friend's gojis are dying, he must be the worst gardener in Britain.'

That was me, the worst gardener in Britain and it stung, deeply. This was the answer on Radio 4's *Gardeners' Question Time* to my friend's question as to why my two goji plants were dying. An accountant where I worked was asking on my behalf but his first mistake was to start his question with, 'My friend', thereby making it seem as though the dying gojis were really his and he was trying to offload his failure on to his friend. Later, he constantly cursed me for his humiliating insult heard by thousands of listeners.

It was clearly my fault and I felt the guilt deeply. But that was the motivation I needed when the Covid-19 lockdown arrived. I was bursting with enthusiasm to dig holes with muddy fingers, order stuff online: plant seeds, plugs and root balls. So, if you're looking to fill your time during lockdown, forget 'Bird-watching from Indoors'; learning French or playing the cello. Just get stuck into growing beautiful flowers and tasty veg.

You know it makes sense.

Born in Liverpool down by the docks, John escaped to the mountains and lakes of North Wales and then hitchhiked around the world for three teenage years before going straight to university and then London.

My Domain by Peter Bendall

My little garden, hardly long enough
for seven strides, confined by ivied wall
and leaning fence composed of fragile stuff,
in which forsythia blossoms gently fall
around the showy primula, and bees
inspect the stamens of the fuchsia bells,
while gradually the sun surmounts the trees
to lend its warmth to multiplying cells
of phlox, camellia and hellebore
that seem in stillness to impart a grave
pronouncement from their enigmatic core,
as if they had the power to damn or save.
This bountiful though limited domain
keeps me, in this emergency, half-sane.

Peter is a retired teacher living in Cambridge and occasionally writes poems.

Green Fingers by Terry Hobson

Imagine how rewarding it must be
to grow your own plants from cuttings and seeds.
Tiny leaves emerging from day to day,
as you feed and water with a gentle spray.
Hours of care with knowing hands
in a greenhouse, garden or piece of land.
Keeping all pests and wild animals at bay
lest they come and chew the foliage away.
A few weeks of patience – then for all to see
a host of pretty flowers in all their glory.
Oranges, reds, purples – every possible hue
with each new dawn a more delightful view.

Terry is retired and divides her time between her families living in the UK and Australia.

The Piece of Thyme by Sheila Johnson

This piece of thyme is all I have left of the time
we spent together in the walled Victorian garden
at Hughenden. We could not touch because of
coronavirus, simply bash elbows for our contact
even though you, my children, adults now,
I longed to hug you, kiss you, hold you with
a mother's love. This virus has separated us.

You in your worlds of computers and medicines
and I in mine, dreaming, thinking, wishing, writing
about what could have been, should have been
if things were normal. But what is normal now
as we live through a pandemic of global proportions?
We laugh and joke and take our photos, socially distanced,
marking the moment, this moment in time when we
walked together, yet spaced apart.

I kiss the air of these embraced moments,
our moments in the sun as I press the piece of thyme
stolen from the garden to my heart
as I would have pressed you if I could.
But the moment now has passed like the thyme.
All I can do now is to hold you in my heart,

praying for better days.

*Sheila has published two novels: 'Alpha Male' and 'Waireka'
under her pen name Sheila Donald. She has also contributed to two
other books: Association of Christian Writers' 'Merry Christmas
Everyone' and a poetry anthology, 'Stones before the Ocean'.*

Further details can be found on Sheila's website at
www.journojohnson.com

Locked Down Daughters by Lois Hambleton

My youngest girl, she wanted Macedonian scabious, the wine red plant that sprawls across my garden. Reminded her of me she said. I laughed, feeling so like my daughter, that bit of brightness that might be a rose, a theatre night. Just like a girl who sings, can hold a note. I think of making tea and eating cake.

My older girl, lives on her own, an attic flat and yet, of all the ladies on this earth she is the one who needs a garden most. Just like a girl who knows her plants, she's of the nettle, meadow rue, the long grass where the barn owl hunts. She called me up to say, *I bought geraniums today, fresh off the supermarket shelf, salmon pink with patterned leaves, they just reminded me of you.* I smiled, feeling so like my daughter, sometimes in pain, a hard built place. I think of Christmas trees and eating cake.

Whittling by Kathyn Wharton

We whittled days,
legs fast and running, short cuts found,
narrow paths and ginnels.
At the top of a town
small roads wound fairy tale white houses,
neat suburban gardens.

What dreams exchanged?
If any they are gone now, legs slow and steady
we take the long route round
noticing light
refract in puddles, birds in autumn houses,
trees already climbed.

Hungry stomachs will take us back to rooms
Polaroid-bright with faces –
a yellow door left open –
a kitchen's orange wall, bones of days
lay unburied at the surface
carve their footprints in the landscape.

Between Jobs by Mary Wiles

Since I retired from paid work 21 years ago, I have been involved in several voluntary roles: at our local church doing gardening, with Rennie Grove working in the shop at Holmer Green on Saturday mornings and also organizing street collections and helping with other events, driving for our local Community Transport scheme, taking people to hospital appointments and also running a club for the elderly at St Michael and All Angels Church in Beaconsfield.

When lockdown started, I saw online, on Facebook that many people were teaching themselves new skills, languages etc. but I really could not get interested in that. I felt quite redundant and useless, not being able to help others and having to submit to being classed as 'vulnerable'. I am 77 and have accepted that people did things for me. By the end of the first lockdown, I can honestly say that all I had achieved was a good suntan!

Mary lives in Prestwood, Buckinghamshire and has been a supporter of Rennie Grove for over 30 years.

I'm Going Viral by Bryn Strudwick

I wrote a poem about current events;
I felt I was duty bound.
But my PC wouldn't accept it.
There's some sort of virus going around.

Cows' Backsides by Chris Sprange

The storm comes
like an explosion
as though the setting sun
has slammed into the Earth.

Shockwaves arrive
as westerly winds
that rattle window panes
carry the scent of cows
from the field next door.

Looking out, bovine backsides
fill the view.
Are these signs
summing up these times?
Everything looks grim
with the situation we are in.

But think again.
When you are seeing bums
and dirt blows in your eye
you are facing
and not fleeing
what is coming your way.

Chris, from rural Leicestershire is using the extra time at home to write poetry and explore the local area with a dog he is fostering through these strange times. He writes: 'The walking isn't quite making up for the extra cooking we've been enjoying though'.

Antibodies and Any Bodies by Dialina Baumann

What antibodies are available to protect us against the bodies that are out there fighting against every and any body? Do the vulnerable have antibodies fighting for them?

Refuse collectors, bakers and administrators – were they the essential antibodies appointed to protect us against the anybodies? Did they know they were special or was it a responsibility that was thrust upon them? Are they more comfortable now that the hairdressers and massage therapists have joined them? Do they feel more protected? Strengthened and bolstered by numbers? What about the medical personnel? Do they need company, or do they miss no one, pleased to attend only to those who truly need them, not distracted by drunken drivers and axe wielding fiends?

And in the meantime, on a beautiful beach in the South Peninsula, the sun was out, the sky was blue, the sea was like a silken lake, and the rest were out at play, not knowing that there was something else out there, something scary that others were very afraid of. As they put their toes into the icy waters and turned their faces to the warm sunlight, they were free, and grateful to be alive.

June 2020

Dialina is from Simon's Town, Cape Town where she lives in awe and gratitude of the absolute beauty that she is surrounded by on a daily basis. She is a member of Fish Hoek Scribblers.

From Cape to Cuba by Charisse Louw

Suddenly it looks like we'll be able to walk outside again in exactly a week's time. I find myself overwhelmed with how little I've accomplished during lockdown. I even made a list to remind myself of what was most important and none of those things has been achieved. Not one. Some I've dabbled in. But mostly I tried to keep our family home clean, the people and animals in it fed, myself from behaving too badly. It turns out domesticity has never been my preferred mode, so why did I think that having the volume turned all the way up would be an invitation to be my Best Self? Managing my anxiety has been more than enough truly. Fortunately my mid-life crisis was in full swing pre-pandemic so the virus can't take all the blame for the incessant silent screaming going on in the echo chambers of my heart and mind. Constantly aware of my privilege: secure home and finances, always looking for ways to help and all that.

But really if this has served as a wake-up call then it's: 'Get the hell out!'

Charisse lives in Noordhoek, Cape Town between the mountains and the sea with three cool cats, a muso husband and two kids who are very forgiving.

Pearls of Wisdom by Jane Edmonds

When I come out of lockdown
I'll stop wiping handles
and walk in gold sandals.

When I come out of lockdown
I'll put rings in my ears
and wear Aphrodite's tears.*

When I come out of lockdown
I'll paint my toenails
and curl my hair.

When I come out of lockdown
I'll wear a floral dress
and stop this idleness.

*'Aphrodite's tears' was an ancient name for pearls.

I Will Wear Lipstick by Nikki Magrath

In the year of Covid-19 lockdowns, many of life's simple pleasures were taken away as we all observed life at a two-metre distance from each other. With my degree of severe hearing loss this instantly became more of a challenge when the wearing of face masks became mandatory.

A good conversation involves active listening, hearing, lip reading and watching visual cues. Take away the ability to *see* what someone is saying and communication breaks down. A face mask destroys the art of conversation.

So how many conversations have I misread? Hundreds if not more. So often I just found myself nodding wisely in agreement hoping that this was the response people were expecting. How I long for the day when people look themselves again and are not obscured by a face covering. In our mask free world, people's faces will light up again and I will stand a much better chance of hearing what they have to say. No date has yet been given for this simple return to 'normality' in the road map that we are following, but rest assured when the day comes, I will be ready with lots of catch-up conversations and lipstick.

Nikki is Marketing Manager at Aston Hearing Services, Buckinghamshire, mother of two children, two dogs and proud to be a hearing aid wearer.

Signature French by Danielle Stevenson

Before it arrived in my life and in spite of my age, I felt young, I thought young, I even acted young.

But suddenly there was a knock at the door. 'Are you over seventy? You are old and in mortal danger: stay at home, stay at home.'

Life changed. I could no longer show off my beautiful cashmere coat or my trendy leather trousers. I ended up living in old jeans and very old clothes. In fact I saved a lot of money as there were no clothes, shoes or handbags to buy and add to my collection.

Was it a good lesson, telling me that clothes are not important? Not at all. It had the opposite effect. I cannot wait to go back to my lovely collection of cashmere sweaters, linen dresses and trousers in many beautiful colours. I want to wear them more than ever. They make me cheerful. They make me feel good. They make me feel alive.

So, Covid-19, you have not won.

Danielle is a 75-year-old Parisienne.

Home by Kadotka Ridwan

The red and white takes flight
on the seventeenth of August.
All so mighty and bright.
Will come back home – you told them – you promised.
Far from home, all alone.
That was almost three years ago.
Free to roam, still alone.
The most you are making of it.
You came here to learn.
No, you came here to live
and you did live life.
Life you have lost before and lives that have been lost.
What should have been your summit.
But looking for a firework
you found a campfire that's dead.
It was damp. So your hands clamp on hope
only for them to loosen off the dry rope.
Things change. You were certain of it.
How big you're uncertain of:
a broken wing, a broken bone,
a broken home, a broken soul.
The nest may be empty
bereft of life.
But the weight you carry
pretty hefty.
Now,
home is wherever I go.
Home is wherever I am.

Kadotka's first language is Indonesian and he is studying Creative Writing at the University of Winchester. An aspiring screenwriter, he is currently trying to balance hours of movies, TV shows, reading and his university work.

Atavistic Campfire by Olivia Rzadkiewicz

When I feel alone sometimes, I like to imagine the campfire. It is a place where my heart goes to find great comfort in knowing my tribe is there at the end of each hard day. We sit around the fire together, whatever has gone between us in the day, and against the blue-black of the sky we are illuminated by a pure light and we see our connection more clearly. We bring to the fire all our hopes, whispered prayers, and consolations. They are fanned into flame. We bring our tears and failures to be extinguished in the quiet presence of hearts glowing in the heat. We make orbits of the sun together, season after season, year after year, good harvest and failed crop. This is the fire my ancestors sat around and where more will come when I'm gone. The meeting point of God and humanity on our journey through the wilderness of life. The mystery of flickering shadows, of fears put to flight.

So when there's a distance between us and the words don't quite seem to fit, look in your heart and you'll find there that the flame has already been lit.

Olivia was born in Manchester but has called Buckinghamshire home since she was nine years old. She works in Marketing and Communications for the National Trust, but likes to dabble with painting and writing to try and make sense of emotions, events and her Catholic faith.

149

Intruders by Jan Moran Neil

We find them in the mornings,
dead under the sills,
not knowing how they have arrived
and search for cracks or holes.
Flying ants; it must be the weather
or something we have done.

We find them in the mornings,
pushed under the slit at our front door:
Birnam Wood to Dunsinane:
flies by some other name with glossy manes
advertising a cruise or new hair salons
where we can spend our pensions.

We find them in the mornings,
sleeking across our screens
begging bank details, screaming alerts.
We flick them, vacuum, press delete,
They stain our silence.

And even in the evenings
silk-edged with soft rain
they come and come again
down the telephone line.
We are confused. How do they get in?
To our home: ordered, white, edited, pristine.

'Intruders' was first published in Jan's collection 'Red Lipstick & Revelations' published by Indigo Dreams and available from her or on Amazon.

Out of Season by Jane MacKinnon

Not yet August, but the leaves are turning.
Through thin cotton shirt, my back is burning.
I'm picking blackberries, ripe in July!
Unless the summer slipped stealthily by
while I slept dreaming to my autumn years.

Time, time – you run out of control,
faster, faster, until my soul begs, 'Stop!'
But no-one hears.

Except, perhaps, that man on Oxford Street,
where, bag-burdened shoppers on weary feet,
we did not pause, we did not catch his eye,
or heed his warning that the end was nigh.
It still was spring for us and way back then
we had no thought of three score years and ten.
Life stretched ahead and time seemed endless.
How soon it would foreshorten and compress
a month to a week, a week to a day.

I'll freeze the fruit to keep the rot at bay.

*Jane is a retired magazine writer and editor, working mainly
for home and consumer magazines, including both British and
Australian 'Good Housekeeping'. She lives with her husband and
dog, with woods and fields on her doorstep. She has no right to
complain.*

Reading the Signs by Tony Turner

A month ago swifts ceased
their shrieking and departed.
Plants are taking longer
to produce returns
and though apples on trees
look rosy, corrupted fruit
litters the ground. Blackberries
glisten darkly on barbed briars,
wasps busy themselves around
like vultures
and evenings chill
as the sun goes down.
Soon wires will be beaded
with dew and swallows
planning to go.

I shall ignore these signs
go on believing in summer
refuse to put on my vest
watch cricket to the final match
admire girls in revealing dresses
go to romantic places
take all the holidays I can
keep on doing those jobs
to be done 'while the good weather lasts'
till the last
possible
moment.

By kind permission of Jeanne Turner. Tony was a first 'Rhyme & Reason' editor (1992-1993) and a valued chair of Metroland Poets. He published five poetry collections including: 'Some I Did Earlier' and 'Reading the Signs'/Cherrycroft Press. He witnessed Roger Bannister break the four minute mile in 1954.

AUTUMN

'THE CHIDING AUTUMN ...'

SHAKESPEARE'S 'A MIDSUMMER NIGHT'S DREAM'

Time for Swallows to Fly South by Syd Neil

When autumn descends on the Northern Hemisphere, the swallows head south to sunnier climes. How they get there with no Air Traffic Control or compass is a miracle. In our own way, my wife and I have been 'swallows' for the last 18 years – making the 6,000 mile journey to Cape Town inside a somewhat larger metallic bird laden with modern technology. Fish Hoek is the nest where I spent my youth before heading north to the UK.

I'm sure the swallows flew out as usual last autumn arriving in the South African spring. It takes them six weeks flying over some very varied terrain: France, Spain, Morocco, crossing the Sahara Desert, the Congo rainforests and Namibia. They fly low and cover 200 miles a day, feeding entirely on flying insects, eating on the wing and snapping up food along the way. We do it in 11 hours at 35000 feet, at night, travelling at nearly 600 miles an hour and grazing on indifferent food. But for us humans the last twelve months have been very different. Lockdowns, lock-ins and locked away.

Holidaying in Cape Town, the swallows have experienced amazing sights en-route and on arrival swooped down, in perfect formation, over a sparkling blue ocean, skimming the waves: enjoying the warm and comforting sun on their backs with the mountains providing a spectacular backdrop. But the swallows too have their challenges. Many die of starvation. Life, for all species on our planet, is sometimes an arduous journey. But the joy and pleasure of arrival is what we all seek.

And returns are sweeter for the waiting.

Syd was born in Cape Town and moved to the UK in his early twenties. He has always been fascinated by the concept of airborne flight. His father was a pilot in the RAF and Fleet Air Arm in the 1940s. Apart from Syd's day job as a finance director of international companies, he learnt to fly light aeroplanes, which he still dreams about.

The Old Normal by Karen Gray-Kilfoil

'Granny, what was it like during the Old Normal?' Ten-year-old Floyd adjusted his mask and waved around the clear Perspex barrier between them.

'Well, we had a lot of adventures. Your grandfather and I flew on aeroplanes like this nearly every year, to different continents. We hiked in South America, took buses in France and shopped in markets in Kathmandu.'

Floyd swept his hand over his forehead, just like his father used to do. Thandi was a good mother, worked hard and helped to pay for Floyd to join her on this expensive trip to Nepal.

'You mean a supermarket, Granny?'

'No. They were crowded. People jostled and haggled. It was fun!'

A white rubber glove handed her a sealed bag containing a plastic-looking sandwich. Was that bread? The white-suited hostess smiled plastically behind her shield.

'But Granny, wasn't it scary being in a crowd with all those germs?'

'No, you had to be aware of pickpockets, but it wasn't scary.'

She remembered how Mike loved to travel, and his last words and still sparkly eyes as they took him out the door in 2020: 'I hope you get to the Himalayas again, when this is all over'.

Karen is a puppy trainer, environmental activist, traveller and occasional writer who lives near Fish Hoek, in Cape Town and manages the writing group Scribblers.

Taking Flight by Meghan Thomas

If snow be the symbol of hope then let it snow on.
If the forest be the symbol of fear and loneliness
then how should one feel trapped in a snowy forest?
Snow drowns out the sound if you ask.
That is how one is expected to cope.

Then there is the autumn; the damp leaves they are all so fawn.
The isolated seasons neglect the homeliness.
Yet the summer months have a longing chorist.

If rain is the relaxer of all weathers then why are storms so tense?
Why does the thunder terrorize the child's innocent soul?
Why does lightning kill?
Some say storms bring us together.
But some souls have no sense.
Some souls don't have the drive or the goal.
Yet why does the eye of the storm remain so still?

If the sun's rays bring joy and goodwill
then let them shine till they can shine no more.
If love is the food of the soul then let the soul feast.
If the bird's feather become the quill
do we then stop the bird from being able to soar?
For the drive and the goal the bird is a magnificent beast.

Meghan is thirteen, currently writing her first novel and studying at Eggars School, Alton in Hampshire. Follow Meghan's author journey on TikTok: @lightbulb_books.

Wings and a Prayer by Robert Rayner

A stallholder stacks a crate of pangolins
next to the bats in Wuhan food market.
Days later the customers awake – coughing.
It goes unnoticed.

In the garden this spring morning
a small tortoiseshell butterfly lies
dead still in the shade as if
pinned and glass-cased.
Its delicate wings are stretched
in perfect petalled symmetry – palette
by translucent orange,
black and yellow hazard spots
and tips ringed by blue crescents.

Hours pass – it waits
for the reach of warming rays.
At last antennae quiver, then a jerky
beating of wings tests the energy store,
before the butterfly rests once more.

Buoyed by a sudden uplift it dances
past daffodils drinking the sun – knows
the course of life is quickly run.
And it is late.
At heather's purple bloom it flits and sips,
giddily, gaudily flutters to deceive a mate.

There are no reports of far-off
hurricanes on the lunchtime news,

just the three-slogan prayer.
So we too pause our lives
and patiently forbear –
easy, let's not pretend.
Earth can convalesce
the atmosphere repair,
and we may dare
believe the chaos will end.

Robert's interests include reading, following Newcastle United, Parkrun and spending time with family. He has achieved success in various writing competitions and in normal times loves to travel and explore the world.

Butterfly Cocoon by Marion Caragounis

The kind of separation that the pandemic has brought to my life could hardly be described as a lockdown. I had already reached an age when adjustments were being made. I had retired to Greece and life had relaxed considerably. My social circle was smaller, there were fewer demands upon my time. I could 'see' family and friends as often as I wanted and when the need to hug became too hard to resist then a visit was made. Perhaps that is why being locked down seemed half way to normal for me and cocooned was a better word.

During lockdown I have received emails from friends with whom I had almost lost touch, asking how I was getting on. Their lives had been put on hold. Formerly their eyes had been on the clock but now we are simply serving time together waiting for the pandemic to pass and their busy lives to start again. Now, as vaccination is available, I may soon need to vacate my cocoon, and prepare for whatever changes may have occurred to me during this time and what changes I will meet outside when this is all over. I am a little afraid that I may have slowed into stop. I have grown used to living in a comfort zone.

A butterfly emerges unable to fly until her wings have dried out and she has flexed them in the sun. I must do the same. I hope I will fly.

When You're Free, Be Free by Katherine Clarke

When you're free, be free, spread your wings and fly.
When you're free, be free, embrace your soul, fly high.

Hold your friends and your family, lean into their souls.
Look deep in their eyes, see their inner troubles and joys.
Hold their hands in yours, let their skin melt your palm.
Feel their heartbeat, hear the sounds of their lives.

Step into your life and play the lead role.
Stop yearning for yesterday, stop waiting for tomorrow.
Touch sadness, drown in happiness, emotions are life's gain.
Drive your destiny, sail your journey, choose your life's frame.

Pause and notice nature, through its wisdom you will find
the essence of who you truly are in spirit and mind.
Care for nature to be kinder to your inner self.
Build a resilient environment, to safeguard your future's health.

When you're free, be free, spread your wings and fly.
When you're free, be free, embrace your soul, fly high.

Katherine lives and works in the beautiful Peak District National Park. She works for the National Trust and tries to inspire people to pause and notice nature, connect with and see themselves as part of nature and make positive changes to their lives; to live more lightly and thoughtfully on the planet for their own benefit and for the benefit of our precious wildlife.

Spaceman by David Keighley

Sometimes I think it very odd,
to find that I believe in God.

For Man has seen with his own eyes
there's nothing there above the skies.

I used to think that very soon
we would find something
beyond the moon.

But travels into outer space,
still won't reveal that divine face.

Far beyond where star lights shine
the space time curve of bright Einstein,
still obscures this God of mine.

Yet,
encouraged by a Dead Sea Scroll,
all I find is a giant Black Hole.

But we must keep up our urgent search
for if we fail,
there is no Church.

Don't search the skies
for the risen Lord anointed,
you will be very disappointed.

I now admit it was quite a blow
to find Heaven not above,
nor Hell below.

God and I are not apart.
He is here,
in my heart.

David is a retired Anglican priest originally from London and spent four decades of ministry in Cornwall and Hampshire. Also a psychotherapist and poet having his first anthology of progressive Christian poems for rebellious Christians, 'Poems, Piety & Psyche'/Resource Publications, published autumn 2020. It is available at Amazon and direct from David at www.davidkeighleywriter.com

Leaving Home by Heather Duffy

With a flick of her ponytail she was gone,
sliding doors of departure to flight of possibility.
Wings soaring, no return booked.
And I am a launch pad, with a splinter in my heart.

A Martian's View of Earth by Andrea Neidle

Far, far away
in time and space
there was a land
for the human race.

They called it Earth,
I don't know why.
All you could see
was sea and sky.

There used to be flowers
and animals too.
But the people there
caught some kind of flu.

Some deadly virus
went everywhere.
It was on the ground
and in the air.

That virus killed billions of lives.
And now Earth's the planet where no one survives.

I visited once but never again.
I didn't like the cold and rain.

Andrea is a writer, blogger and poet living in Bushey, Hertfordshire. She is happy to read her work to local groups – on Zoom if necessary. www.andreaneidle.wordpress.com

From a Different Planet by Tinaya Wathudura

Dear Mrs Mars,

I would like to inform you about Earth. I live on planet Earth, where life and ecstasy are filled to the brim. My name is Tinaya and I go to the Breakspear School in Ickenham – which is a town. School is a place where humans endeavour various things and learn the aspects of life. Hobbies that I am enthralled by are reading, writing and dancing: all which I immensely enjoy when I am in solitude. Hobbies are pastimes: they are activities that make one captivated when somebody is feeling tedious.

Writing is primarily the activity that I relish the most. It is diverting and lets you express your feelings. I engage in numerous competitions about poems and stories as I love writing.

The last nine months have been problematic, however also manageable. We have been on lockdown, which is when everybody has to stay indoors until permitted to come out. A deadly virus has been dispersing rapidly. As a result of this irking incident, my exams have been impeded. The advantage of been imprisoned in our houses, is that I have time to practise my writing skills which has truly been exceedingly beneficial.

Captured, the walls locking me in every day.
No glimpse of sunlight snakes through this day.
The windows are shut, we are breathing dense air.
Staying inside is more than we can bear.
Happiness limited, nothing to do.
Cramped in small spaces with nowhere to move.

Tinaya is a year 6 pupil and is ten years old.

Harmony by Louise Moss

The planet is a living, sentient thing that develops and changes. It looked after itself for thousands of years before humans evolved, and continues to do so. By creating a virus that spreads easily amongst humans, Nature halted activities across the world and did more for climate change than we could achieve in years.

If our actions continue to destroy the planet's atmosphere, the next thing could be a virus that kills off a large percentage of the population. If we want to survive, we need to make a significant shift in the way we think about our relationship with the planet.

People make token gestures – recycling, putting a bug hotel in the garden – but continue turning their gardens into car parks, pouring weed killer on their plants, travelling across the world and purchasing the latest fashion and technology – but it is not enough. We must lose the desire for designer handbags and trainers, foreign holidays, bigger televisions, manicured gardens and fresh raspberries in December.

They all contribute to climate change. We must learn to live in harmony with Nature and the Universe or lose everything we hold dear.

Louise is a writer, musician, grandmother, founder of Writers against Covid-19, and is from Kent.

Blue Crystal Dolphins by Hayley Liversidge

They weren't really crystal blue, only in my imagination. In fact they were shimmering grey, as they glided effortlessly in the cyan waters of the Venetian canals. This had never been seen in Venice before. The waters were usually a muddied green, churned up by boats. Now quiet and clean even snow white swans could be seen floating along these ancient waterways.

In the UK our carbon footprint was reduced by two-thirds. With few cars on the road and planes grounded, the air smelt fresh. A farmer near Heathrow heard a nightingale sing. For the first time its song was not drowned out by the drone of aircraft engines.

We can't go back to what it was. There's been too much pain and sacrifice for that. The blue crystal dolphins represent hope in a troubled world. Hope that we work together for a cleaner healthier environment for all.

Hayley has completed a creative writing course with the 'Writers' Bureau' and had articles published in 'Woman Alive' magazine, the local community newspaper and most recently in the online 'MIMAzine'. She has been shortlisted in the 'Crossing the Tees' Short Story Competition and in the 'Writing Magazine' short story competitions.

It by Joanna Wallace

When this is all over …
the sun will still shine.
Not because it's someone's wedding or a bank holiday.
It will just shine.

The mountains will still be.
Not because of the views and potential for selfies.
They will just be.

The sea will still move.
Not because the beach stores are selling surfboards.
It will just move.

The earth will still turn.
Not because Christmas needs to follow Halloween.
It will just turn.

Something else will still decide.
Not because we've made mistakes and can't be trusted.
It will decide.

Joanna is a mother, wife, dog owner and yoga-loving Reiki master from Chalfont St Peter, Buckinghamshire

Time to Pause by Anita Louise Jay

Will life be the same when this is all over? Will we return to our usual self-absorption? I believe the world in which we find ourselves has never in times past remained in stasis. History has proved that change is inevitable and brings forth both upheaval and creation.

We can only trust that the aftermath of this virus accomplishes co-operation amongst world leaders, to tackle climate change, abuse and inequality. As we pause to ponder how our lives have altered maybe we will come to the realization that we can, given the will, uplift the disadvantaged, feed the hungry and make the world a better place for our children. Possibly the curse of Covid will allow us the time we need, to take stock, show gratitude, appreciate Nature's beauty.

Anita is a qualified speech, drama and dance teacher. Her short stories and poetry have been published online and in magazines. She has been an active member of the West Coast Writers, Cape Town for several years. www.moondancestudio.tumblr.com.

Next Time by Pamella Laird

Will there *ever* be an 'Over'?

According to those who know, the world of 2020 will have a population of eight billion! If Earth had a voice, it would cry, 'This cannot go on. I cannot sustain such a weight of humans, plus their despair'. It would be great if we'd learned that a Covid-19 pandemic is Nature's way of creating our clean, fresh air. That internationally we decide we really *don't* need more 'infernal' combustion engines? And, yes! We can all grow our own natural bounty of fruit and vegetables, corn and grain.

Soon we'll have Vaccine Day and Covid-19 will scuttle into the deepest darkest corners. And, all over the world, we'll breathe together, one huge sigh of relief, run into the streets to hug and cheer, just like the end of World War Two. Freedom at last! Now we begin the long road back to reconstruct what used to be our 'normal' lives; of doing what we can to stay alive in a world that before too long will once more, show its despair.

Next time, will it be tsunamis, hurricanes, floods, fires, or another dreaded pandemic that engulfs, once again, our selfish, hedonistic lives?

Pamella is a retired nurse who has travelled round the world seven (seven not several!) times and lives in Orewa, Auckland, New Zealand.

Simplicity by Harriet Mills

When this is all over I'll appreciate more. A trip to town, a mini-break at the beach, a hug, a social gathering, dinner with those I see the most, and dinner with those I see the least. I'll notice nature, let it bring happiness whenever I need it. The natural and pure. Children and mothers, wildlife, trees, grasses blowing in summer breeze, colours of lavender fields and smells of pollen.

I will enjoy sleep knowing now what it is to be deprived of it. Whenever I feel on top form and full of energy I will give thanks, for so long I have been run down during lockdown. Clear skin showing my radiance as opposed to spotty stress. A spring in my step and a smile on my face rather than clumping along with a frown.

Never again will I moan about slowness under pressure while waiting. Instead I will understand the meaning of pressure and give staff a break. I'll try not to worry about money. I'll endeavour to be kind.

When this is all over I'll appreciate freedom we can so easily be denied. Lockdown 2020 – back to basics, simplicity and a love for life.

Harriet has published her debut novel 'Dear Brannagh' which is available on Amazon and Waterstones. Instagram @harrietmillswriting and website www.harrietmills.co.uk

Turning by Charlotte Caine

Having lived through apartheid, the Zuma years and now the pandemic, we still remain in a very segregated society in South Africa: huge differentiation between the haves, the have-nots and those who have lost everything, heightened by rampant government corruption and 'reverse racism' in education and employment opportunity.

I have also survived enormous personal tragedy with the loss of three sons: one soon after birth; my older son (chess champion and BSc graduate), who succumbed after a 25-year battle with drug addiction; and my younger son (two degrees) who, at age 42, suddenly collapsed in a shop and could not be resuscitated.

But we must never lose sight of the disaster and heartbreak resulting from those who have not survived the pandemic. We are grateful for having lived through it – and because of it, becoming more compassionate and mindful. What may have appeared to be the very worst of what nature could inflict on us, may conversely have had a way of bringing out the best in us – and a much-needed turn-around in attitude and understanding of the world in general.

Charlotte worked for a local newspaper, wrote advertising copy, was a market research supervisor and finally, an investment consultant for a large company. She has been the winner of several writing and poetry awards.

Restrictions by Cassandra Van Niekerk

Lockdown in South Africa has five levels with level five being the strictest with only essential businesses operating and level one with nearly all the economy open. Masks are mandatory when going to shops and even walking outside, hands need to be sanitized at every entrance and we are still enduring this since March 2020. Compared to other countries, South Africa has not been as strict but we have done our best and are still trying.

Living in South Africa can be challenging with water restrictions, which also has levels restricting when you can and can't use water and the amount of water each person is allowed per day is also rationed. Rolling blackouts, or load shedding as we call it, occurs due to the capacity of the grid being outstripped by the demand of electricity. Depending on your area and the demand, you could go a while with no load shedding and then having it several times a day for several hours at a time.

We Capetonians have got used to restrictions.

Cassandra studied Conservation Studies (Historic Buildings) and although she would have loved to stay in the UK, Covid-19 ruined these plans and she had to come back to South Africa and go into lockdown just over two months later. She plans to move back to the UK by Christmas 2021 and work in the conservation field if possible.

Masquerade by Alison Milner

I select a mask carefully from the rack in my wardrobe. White clouds printed on layers of grey cotton because it matches today's sky, drizzling a palette of disappointment. I have masks for every mood. My neighbour 'runs' them up.

'It's no trouble,' she says on the phone, sitting hunched over her sewing machine.

The empty pavements of the town glisten early morning damp, like an echo, as I walk to the supermarket. I do not venture out much, but I need some milk. I hear the virus breathe mortality, making potential murderers of the people I pass at a wary distance on the street. The car park is deserted, a tarmac blank. The trolleys are in orderly rows like a chain-gang before work. The clean litter bin is open-mouthed, expectant.

Inside a woman perches behind a glass screen. A gloved hand emerges holding the card payment machine. I tap it, nod a silent greeting and depart quickly. My mask is my sanity. It is washed safe, frequently. It is sterile, cleansed of expression.

Wearing my mask means I only need to control my eyes. They feel like snail tentacles exploring a world as fragile as my shell.

Alison lives in Hebden Bridge, West Yorkshire. She started writing creatively two years ago after early retirement.

Turn, Turn, Turn by Linda Storey

'For everything there is a season, and a time for every purpose under heaven.'

The passage continues, 'a time to weep and laugh, break down and build up, mourn and dance, keep silent or speak'. Each season has its appropriate opportunity in our cycle of life.

A monstrous episode moved us to dig deeper into our energies and hearts to proceed and maintain some sort of balance and sanity. To live our life without closeness of family, and exist through a permanent barrier, was deprivation taken to its limits. Emotions, unknown aptitudes, creativity and compassion erupted. A gift of time was on loan.

This immediate interval allowed an awakening, both mentally and physically; acknowledging new life, community, colours, scents and sounds, both visually and artistically. Long temperate days, eventually dwindled to heartache like leaves that fall too easily to the ground.

My time is not on loan, it is to be used befittingly. Only when this *is* all over will we understand the full impact of TURN, TURN, TURN – a phrase taken from biblical verses, which became a beautiful song.

'TURN' is to move in a circular direction and begin the next season of our life.

Skin by Carolyn Fitzpatrick

My skin no longer fits; draped
across a chair, it pools messily
on to the floor.

I shake it roughly, trying
to dislodge creases and wrinkles
that are permanent fixtures

before stepping in cautiously
to bunions and calloused heels,
toenails thick with age.

I pull on a purple latticework
of veins that decorate my legs
like lacy tights, straining to

encompass puckered knees;
thighs pitted, a lunar landscape,
cellulite craters and troughs.

I drag the quivering mass over
hips widened by childbirth,
stretch marks fork like

lightening across a sagging
stomach; no amount of tugging
will reveal a waist.

I heave it up and over ponderous
breasts, hanging low and heavy,
adorned with rich brown moles.

Round shoulders shelter a butterfly
tattoo weeping rivulets of purple ink.
An awkward wriggle into

batwing arms that hang as if
stuffing has been removed; hands
slip into crocodile gloves.

Rolling up a crepey neck on to the face
that is not mine, eyes peer
between a myriad of wrinkles and

liver spots, crow's feet indented by
a lifetime of smiles and frowns.
No longer tight or toned

or firm or trim, everything has stretched
like old elastic; worn, well used,
comfortable as brushed cotton pyjamas.

*Carolyn was born in Ealing, west London, and moved to
Buckinghamshire in 1988 where she is now an 11 plus tutor for
entry into the Buckinghamshire grammar schools.*

Beauty at a Distance by Jane MacKinnon

The brightness of birdsong,
distant baa-ing of sheep –
these are the sounds that wake me from,
and lull me into, sleep.

And I sink back and think:
all's well with the world.

But the feathered breast swells to threaten a fight,
and the bleats are from dams
who have lost their lambs and cry through the night.

These creatures call through worry and grief,
yet as I listen, I feel at peace.

Perhaps there is another self, distant in the universe,
who hears with joy the diverse noise rising from our earth.
The chit-chat chatter of the battle guns,
sweet keening of those who sob for their sons.

Does she, like me, sink back and think:
all's well with the world?

And when our planet is no more –
light years ahead of where we are –
my soul, on hearing its dying roar,
will see the brilliance of our falling star.

Will she, like me, sink back and think:
all's well with the world?

Amalfi Lemons by Barbara Pavey

I puff my way to the top
through aged pathways
and cobbled streets.
Narrow steps wind upwards around quaint houses
where locals peer through shuttered windows
and sunlight casts mysterious shadows.
Geraniums smile from window boxes
and laundry floats above the alleys.
An archway beckons
and clock tower stands sentinel.
I wander into the piazza
where generations mingle with pipe smoke and banter;
where visitors embrace the outdoor traditions of
congeniality
and enjoy fresh-cooked fare from the season's storehouses.
I wander to the lemon grove
and pick the oval teardrop.
I feel the pitted surface,
cut into the pithy flesh
and inhale its acidic fragrance.
Its free spirit oozes out
    and juices my palate.

A Statistic by Cristina de Lama

I have a superpower.

I am invisible.

I can walk naked around the house and nobody bats an eye.

Outside the house I'm invisible too. I'm not a part of any of the statistics that counts these days. I'm not a kid, I don't go to school; I'm no pensioner either. I'm not married, I have no children. I don't work, I'm neither teleworking nor furloughed; I'm a self-employed or, rather, self-non-employed. I'm not a key worker, I don't save lives, help lives, look after lives, feed lives. I'm not BAME. I'm not religious. I don't drink, I don't do drugs. I'm sure of my gender. I read! Does that count? I'm not 'vulnerable'. Well, I am but, at the same time, I am not. I vote when I can, when I'm allowed to.

Wait: there's one statistic I can be part of. I'm an EU citizen living in the UK! During a pandemic! So ... sure, I'm still invisible. An invisible white EU middle-aged woman who used to work in the arts and now is unemployed. Isolated. A year without a family, a kiss or a hug.

But I've still got my voice.

Cristina is Spanish but has been living in High Wycombe, Buckinghamshire for the past fifteen years. She is a freelance sound engineer who works in theatre, opera and broadcasting ... or used to, until a year ago. She loves reading, movies, travelling, languages, nature and tennis.

Getting the Right Forms in Place by Avra Kouffman

I am single in my 50s – not yet old but not a young adult, either. This pandemic showed me it's time to start 'taking care of business'. My landlord, who lives on-site, insisted his renters should not expect his help if we caught Covid. He asked us to put emergency contacts on the fridge and said the contacts we chose would need our medical information. I created an emergency plan, typed it up, and shared it with three friends. Then I realized I would need an Advance Health Care Directive with a Medical Power of Attorney. This form takes different names from place to place, but the main idea doesn't change much. If you're incapacitated, your Medical Power of Attorney is responsible for making life-and-death decisions about your care. In California, we also choose two alternates. It can take time to find the right people and discuss the idea with them. Then the form must be notarized. A copy is now taped to the back of my bedroom door. Several months into the pandemic, I feel reasonably prepared, paperwork-wise, should Covid-19 come my way. I appreciate that my friends are kind, caring, and willing to help.

Avra is a writer in southern California, USA. She has done a lot of travelling, teaching, performing, and adapting to life outside her hometown, New York City.

Contrasts in a Pandemic by Jürgen Dankwort

Here on the west coast of Canada, I've tried to make the best of a pandemic crisis, mindful of my privileged life as a formally educated white male, surrounded by supernatural wilderness on a peninsula called the Sunshine Coast, with all the essentials anyone could hope for, unlike millions experiencing daily hunger and living in squalor.

Initially gripped by sleepiness bouts and stomach-cramping anxiety at the breaking daily news, I soon saw grocery shelves quickly replenished and health-care managing the stricken, starkly contrasting the lives of refugees and homeless elsewhere. I could carry on my contacts virtually with friends, unlike those in solitary confinement, identified as torture by Amnesty International. I continued working on my projects as before from my home office, retired and free from concerns of unemployment, so different from those most affected by Covid loss, mostly women, persons of colour.

And I reflected continually on the bravery and courage of all frontline workers even after the pots and pans fell silent several months into last spring, thanking checkout clerks for keeping us alive, the physician still able to see me, tipping the barber more generously when haircuts reappeared.

I thought kudos to all who demonstrated collective responsibility and accepting physical distancing, refusing to chance becoming a virus transmitter even in the face of duplicitous politicians who fled to their resorts while making their stay-at-home and non-essential travel dictums for the rest of us.

But how long this mindfulness of darkness and light will enrich my appreciation after the jabs have been done, that is the question, isn't it?

Jürgen lives in Sechelt, British Columbia, Canada. PhD researcher, author, educator, activist. For details and contact: www.ivsi.net

Working in the Townships by Earl Albert Mentor

The emergence of the Covid-19 virus across our communities has brought us under a great deal of strain. I have witnessed how this form of stress has brought the many communities and participants we serve, under the auspices of our charity organization *www.mentoringpeacebuilders.org,* to the breaking point. This has resulted in a large number of mental health problems. The Covid-19 pandemic and the economic recession have negatively affected many people's mental health and has created new barriers for people already suffering from mental illness and substance use disorders within the communities we serve. We have witnessed that many of our beneficiaries are experiencing specific negative impacts on their mental health and well-being. Sadly the overwhelming challenges around parents' job losses and food insecurity have accelerated depression, anxiety, distress, and low self-esteem amongst the vast majority and we in turn have personally witnessed how these difficult situations have led to higher rates of substance abuse and attempted suicide.

It has been a tough year, but we remain positive and enthusiastic about what the New Year brings. We are indeed stronger and powerful as ever.

January 2020/Approaching autumn in South Africa.

Earl is an Anti-Bias and Racial Equity Facilitator and Solution Focused Life Coach offering cultural workshops and seminar-style life coaching sessions. He lives in the township Ocean View, Cape Town and is author of 'Cape Flats Karma Bocs' available on Amazon.

Working from Home by Rob Shipman

Working from home is about watching pigeons in the sunshine riding each other. There they are on the roof of the house opposite visible from the back bedroom. Sending messages on a group chat about nothing and not really getting a reply. Speaking with a colleague who needs to talk as lives alone. Seeing the dog get on her bed conditioned by the sound of pouring coffee, her eyes full of the forlorn hope of a biscuit.

Working from home is about the same 'good morning' shared on group chat. The self-motivated desire to get the task done. The excitement at another delivery, and the dog hitting the kitchen door with rampant ferocity. A melancholy musing about how Monday mornings used to be.

Working from home is full of the resonance of newscasters: 'It will never be the same again!'

My pondering as to what that means, knowing every day is defined and shaped by its predecessor.

I have a familiar cycle route, a programme of foods, a timetable of coffee breaks uninterrupted by a shared worker.

Working from home is a Venn diagram of overlapping activities trapped inside a bubble.

I *really* have had enough of it! I think I could have a job working from home, but my job was never that, it could never be that! I will be glad when we move into another time, but will be grateful for the stop.

We flow through life, and sometimes, a stop, is what we need to recognize the fast disappearing scenery.

Rob is 52 years old and works for Citizens Advice as a paid worker answering calls. He lives with his wife, teenage son and crazy Staffy Patterdale called Bronte (she is from Yorkshire).

Left Behind by Penny Black

I will sit in church halls rehearsing day after day,
uncomplaining of awful acting, terrible coffee,
cheap biscuits, uncomfortable chairs, impractical
set design.

I will go to the theatre night after night,
uncomplaining of high prices, queues for the bar,
coughing in the stalls, rustling in the upper circle,
no legroom.

I will invite my friends round for huge dinner parties
not caring if my food is not gourmet, the room overcrowded,
the plates not matching, or the fact that someone brought
two children and a dog who ends up vomiting
behind the sofa.

I will walk slowly down the street, savouring the sun
or the rain, or the hail or the sleet – will I care?
I will greet neighbours and friends, stop to chat, walk
the old lady across the road, pat the dog, rescue the cat,
before walking on.

I will squeeze and hug and kiss everyone I can who does not
mind.
Not caring they have a cold, they look embarrassed – I won't
care.
And we will hang on to each other like grim death, the left
behind,
knowing that we are the lucky ones, we, the left behind.
The left behind.

Penny is a translator and playwright. Her one-woman show about Gustav Klimt's muse, Emilie Floege (the woman in 'The Kiss') has been seen in museums and theatres all over the world.

See Paris in the Autumn by Martine Couffinhal

I am a Parisian and a lover of England. It is with interest that I have followed the development of the pandemic on each side of the Channel. These are my observations: amazed, worried and frustrated. France was in lockdown while Boris and his mop of blond hair was going from one meeting to another, shaking hands with happy Covid-infected Brexiteers, drinking pints of beer without care with his pals. Then Boris disappeared into a hospital as the virus dived on the English like the Stuka Nazi war planes on London. We were really sorry ...

But our lovely summer ended and we were subjected to a semi-confinement and moaned at the curfew and shop closures, as our dear friends (?) the English, gave us two presents: the vaccine and the variant. We were vexed by the first and furious with the other. Finally we were grateful for the former and bore the other. Being well-known philosophers we thought that at least we had escaped Megxit and Meghan Markle's shenanigans

Long live the Queen!

Martine is a Parisian and lover of England.

Kissing Oceans by DL Lang

When it is safe I shall run to hug my friends,
grateful for their smiling faces.
I shall revel in communal experiences
from the county fair to the theatre.
I shall kiss the oceans and the forests,
having missed them from the safety of home.
I shall be grateful for having survived this.
I shall fondly remember those who did not.

DL Lang was born in Germany, reared in Texas, Louisiana, and Oklahoma, and currently resides in Vallejo, California, USA where she served as Poet Laureate from 2017 to 2019.

Taste, Touch and Turn by Maureen Bradley

Our taste of life we know has paused
that much is very true,
so much is out there for us all
to reconnect anew.
Simple joys that touch your heart and soul
as we keep on yearning,
but no matter how we feel this day,
the world will keep on turning.

Giving Thanks by Rose Chaffé

I consider myself extremely fortunate.

Luck has it, I took the plunge to leave full time work and qualify as a mountain leader one year before the pandemic arrived. Pairing this outdoor qualification with my previous experience, I have been able to temporarily leave London and work from the Lake District these last few months. Hiking is my passion: it has enabled me to be in the outdoors, staying fit in mind and body, and learn fundamental survival skills. Away from the city, people and visual reminders of restrictions, we have cocooned ourselves in nature.

This time has made me feel grateful. Grateful for the friends I have, my financial situation, my partner and my age in life. I've not missed the university years, London partying in my twenties, nor been of older years and therefore extra cautious.

I know it will be all the sweeter when I see my friends for not having seen them for so long.

I hope my gratitude stays with me.

Rose is from Tunbridge Wells, Kent and now lives in west London with her partner Stu. They are soon to move to New Zealand for eighteen months, to travel the country and wait out what is left of this pandemic.

Thanking by Claire Keogh

When this is all over I will sing and dance,
and eat ice-cream and burgers with my friends and
hug my family and go to the cinema
and never take home deliveries or healthcare
for granted again.
I will thank my nurse for calling out to see me
from behind her mask and sunglasses
to keep me safe,
to keep her safe.

To give me vital medicine and treatment
because I was cocooning.
I will thank her over and over
for all the lives she saved,
for all the lives she's saving.
Her and all the team.
Thank you HSE and NHS and all the teams
and hospitals the world over.

I will pray, like I've never prayed before.
When the churches open,
I will be thankful for the pew and the silence
and the candle and the wooden seats
and the host and the priest
who could have died for me.
For you, for us.

For the moment,
I am thankful for the streaming
of the Mass and the news,

the internet, the technology
that makes our safety possible:
the men and women
that make our safety possible.
Thank you all.

Claire is a writer from Dublin, Ireland who loves to cook and travel and has recently retired from public service employment. She writes poetry, fiction and non-fiction and has published five books on Amazon.

Separation by Chris McDermott

Lockdown says that our lives have been halted. Physically, that is true. But do we inhabit our body or do we inhabit our mind? Can our body feel happiness and sadness, regret and hope?

No.

It is our bodies that transport us to places where we can have those feelings, but it is our minds that create those feelings. Talking to someone via our computer is not the same as giving that person a hug, but it is a gift that we have that generations before could only dream of. How many times have we heard people complain that work gets in the way of living? Now we have that time for our minds to reflect, to create, to remind us how much we love those dear to us. Just as the starving person craves food and the poor person craves money, it is only by being separated that we truly understand how much we want to be together.

So, thank you for this chance of life, this chance to reflect and feel our true feelings, knowing who we are and who we love. Our loved ones may live outside our building, but they will never live outside our hearts.

Chris's mother Marjorie spent some time in care towards the end of her life. He dedicates these few words to her. Chris was a head teacher, is a writer, a husband, a father and now a grandfather.

Yesterday's Tomorrow by Lynn Noone

Today may be yesterday's tomorrow.
This virus is now testing physical and mental health.
Equalizing all regardless of wealth.
Earth, the sea and air are greatly benefitting
from humans not flying but just endless sitting.
Clear blue skies and birds that sing.
Who knows what tomorrow will bring?
I had plans I am sure you did too.
Visitors are no longer passing through.
Friends and family just images on a screen.
This is the loneliest I have ever been.
I live alone so I have practised talking to walls.
When this was enforced how I longed for calls.
There are consequences if you fail to heed advice
so wait for the world to be normal and nice.
Except normal will never be as it used to be
for when we meet I need space you see.
Give thanks if you are healthy.
Try your best not to moan.
Some of us cry daily for we live on our own.
When this is all over my world will be brand new.
A timeless twisted tunnel of torment will not be my only view.
I intend to observe distance, maintain hygiene, wear a mask.
All are beneficial. Not a lot to ask.

Lynn is 64 years of age and has been isolated for 99 days.

Today's Concerto by Richard Candy

Every day is truly beautiful.
It's the best of our beginning.
The sunrise of the glorious moment
that declares the world is winning.

I want to sing the greatest music,
the monumental force of song.
I want to celebrate every symphony
as everyone battles on.

Never is there such raw intensity
when Beethoven's Ninth does start.
It fills me with determined energy
to write volumes from the heart.

It's at this moment that I bellow
my greatest song of thunder.
Thanksgiving to all the NHS
for the rainbow we stand under.

And it's to that courageous doctor
who battles and persists forever
to eradicate Covid-19
defining true endeavour.

While I think of Bach and Sibelius:
composers I thank in verse,
the soloist in today's concerto
shall be every unheard nurse.

They are Beethovens of our modern medicine,
true Shakespeares of the heart.
I must stand humble, yet I'm inspired
by the symphony they start.

For every fortissimo of the orchestra
prepares the joy forever.
We're going to beat this wretched virus
and we'll do it all together.

Richard is a puzzle designer, 53, now living in Dalkeith, near Edinburgh, Scotland. He has written many short stories and poems as well as one novella and a number of stories for children which he illustrates.

Take Stock by Willow Norbron

When this is all over, we will all come out and cheer,
we'll be dancing in the long lost streets parading with a beer.
The children will be singing as they run to hug their friends,
astonished by their change in face and funky hairstyle trends.

When this is all over, we will embrace each other tight,
taking not for granted holding loved ones through the night.
One kiss that lasts a moment, forever etched in mind,
a heartfelt squeeze, a warm caress so missed from all
mankind.

When this is all over, we will sing our heartfelt song,
praising all the NHS that helped us to be strong.
All the unsung heroes, we never will forget,
providing the necessities, ensuring our needs were met.

When this is all over, I hope we all take stock,
to not take life for granted, who knows when death might
knock?
To treat the earth with kindness as before we were blind to
see
that what has been beneath our feet,
is a wondrous place to be.

*Willow lives in Stoke Poges, Buckinghamshire along with her
husband, two boys, a cat and a dog.*

Alone by Pamela Cavendish

How do I fill in the hours in my long lockdown day?
And how long will we live our lives in this restrictive
lockdown way?
The professional pundits seem to say
it's best to have a structured lockdown day.
I text, I phone and email to say
yes I'm fine in my elderly way.
And how about you?
I do my chores, I polish and clean.
The house is the cleanest it's ever been!
I read, I paint and sing off key
whilst in the bath I watch TV
and sigh ...
But the sun is shining, my spirits lift,
into my garden I will drift
to admire the flowers, colours and birds
singing the sweetest songs you have ever heard.
And I give thanks to those who work so hard
to provide us and nurse us and tell us to guard
against a roving virus which in its virulent way
has caused us all to have a lockdown day.

Pamela is a senior citizen, living in Bourne End,
Buckinghamshire and mercifully, she says, still has some of her
faculties. She enjoys her family, friends, the arts and her garden
and can't wait to give someone a hug.

Clouds, Birds, Trees by Simon Baynes

I stare at clouds.
All day they sail
over our heads
in solemn beauty.
Praise God for clouds.

I marvel at birds,
blessing of the fifth day,
a gift to Man
so beautiful
I have no words to say.
Praise God for birds.

I gaze at trees
in endless reverie
lost in their growing life
greater, older than me:
God's gift to Man
sustaining our brief life.
Praise God for trees.

Power beyond praise,
beauty beyond words,
grace beyond grace. Praise God
for clouds and trees and birds.

Simon is a C of E minister, former missionary in Japan. Father of three, grandfather of eight and is a member of the Association of Christian Writers.

Covid Belfast by Esther Estar

When I was growing up here it was a different kind of fear.
Sadly lives were lost at a bitter cost.
One day we stood hand in hand, made peace in this beautiful
land.
Yet here we are fighting Covid: an invisible war that frightens
us to the core.
Some people think Government is lying yet so many people
are dying.
I've grown angel wings, wrap them round my mother as she
sings
protecting her like a baby.
To master this disaster we need to live by the rules
and those who don't are self-centred fools.
Covid-19 has shown us that no one is safe: no colour, no
religion, no race.
It's shown us we are all the same living in this mental pain
living in this fear, praying it isn't near.

There's a saying that's been around for years ringing in my
ears.
Your health is truly your wealth.
God bless us all, but most of all, God bless the NHS
trying to help those survive, risking their own lives:
Angels on Earth.

*Esther is from Belfast, Northern Ireland and has had a career in
Dance, winning the British Championships, All-Ireland
Championships Dublin, Open Ulster and Coca-Cola
Championships.*

201

A Day in the Life of ... Doctor Jon

When the Covid pandemic broke, a day in my life as a doctor was a peculiar experience. Following a walk to work through the eerily quiet streets I would be greeted by the hospital PPE police. Here I received my daily shake down ensuring my mask was on and that no precious visors were being smuggled down my pants. This act of desperation was a necessity having been caught on the back foot with a lack of supplies. You could feel the tension as managers were forced to frantically search Deliveroo for any 'buy one get one free' deals on protective gowns.

Work began with an obligatory briefing to relay the umpteenth iteration on infection control measures. Although well meaning, these left my head spinning and often felt as effective as rubbing crystals in a vain attempt to cease the onslaught. My phone is buzzing throughout as everyone is proselytizing the latest pandemic management fad generated from yet another shoddy study.

Yet despite all the uncertainty, there was a strong sense of unity which did not exist before, and along with a newfound public respect, it was this which kept everyone coming back for more.

Jon is a medical doctor in Brighton.

Pitch and Toss by Robert Rayner

Each day for an hour
we escape along the track; edge
furrowed fields birds scour,
fill our pockets with posies.

Four seats apart at the funeral,
pocketfuls of memories empty.
Like the poem that slips away –
not what I meant to say.

On Thursdays from living rooms
lit by television glow
socially distanced neighbours emerge;
Clap for Carers, wave hello.

Always in my pocket
a coin and gel –
it's heads for heaven
and tails for hell.

Uncertainty by Rosemary Gray

In these times we are uncertain
facing the world with pandemic flu,
wondering whether we'll be safe
in isolation, hidden from view.
I hold tightly on to the cross in my pocket,
my fear dissolves and I pull out
quickly, more confident and self-assured
thinking what would Jesus do.

Some of us may pray for more life,
really pray to a God who keeps us safe,
but only He knows whether it's our time
to live or to die, no one else can know.

I thank God for our NHS and pray
for those workers taking risks every day
to save us from our own destruction
but I know people will fall sometimes.

He knew God has a plan for this life.
He lived to spread good news to the poor,
to proclaim freedom for us all, so let's live
in his promises, to love and hold on.

Blessed with this time, let's enjoy life
to the full, dig deep into your soul and pray
that you can make a difference, spread
a little kindness to people along the way.

Rosemary is from Newcastle upon Tyne, known by her grandchildren as 'Curly Wurly Grandma'.

The Gospel of Covid-19 by Laura Sansom

I hope that if we were to rewrite the rule books: books by previous icons and existing idols; the kind written by those writers who have led miracle moments and medical achievements, revolutions, and changes to the systems, both actual, physical, and social – I hope in amongst all that content maybe Covid-19 needs to have a piece noted, rewritten, edited or an added appendix?

Whatever the way we choose to document the year that was the pandemic 2020 to 2021 it needs its own highlight, its own showcase in the new history books. Not for the atrocities worldwide but for those who fought hard to keep going, stiff upper lip and muddling on. The Gospel in which the people who once in a certain 'career culture' used to be forgotten are now wonderfully remembered for their part in the pandemic. They were and always should have been celebrated and should never be forgotten beyond this newish year.

It should be a new rule, new law, new scripture, a new song not to ever be unsung that we remember the effort of all frontline workers, our heroes in the Gospel of Covid-19.

Laura has worked in social care for the last twenty years. She writes: 'The last twelve months perhaps being the hardest I have ever experienced in my role as a housekeeper/line manager and a health and safety representative (residential setting)'.

The Key Worker by Carol Fenwick

Delicate hands that change bed linen, empty bins, remove coffee cups.
Patch up patients, clean wounds, warm hearts.
You might not sing songs or write words on paper.
Your words are the hands, the treasure,
the gold dust, the vessel.
I tell you the tale of the emergency worker,
as if it were my own. But it's your story, your unique journey.
From a friend's son who works with autistic kids,
to the student doctors facing fears for the first time.
The distributors who live in hospitals supplying PPE,
to the industrious cleaner and the lady on the desk at beck and call.
The check-out man or woman, the postal workers and lorry drivers.
The teachers, carers, doctors and nurses all on the frontline
who work tirelessly and timelessly for our benefit.
Your words, your hands.

Carol is an author and a poet from Kent.

Lending an Ear by Heather Duffy:
Volunteer 'Listener' within the Family Support Team at
the Rennie Grove Hospice Care.

We are not counsellors but have been through Rennie Grove training to provide active listening support to patients, carers and the bereaved. We try to offer empathy, unconditional acceptance and support as they come to terms with their loss. Under normal circumstances we would visit the homes of the people we are supporting but during Covid most of this has been over Zoom or via the telephone.

So when this is all over we will see our clients face-to-face once more. We will sit side by side and listen to their memories, helping them to move forward through their sorrow, loneliness and fear. We will forget the mask, the screen and the telephone and connect in the warmth of human contact. We will be able to offer a friendly touch or a comforting hug.

When this is all over we will be present, not virtual. We will talk about the people who have been lost and bring them into the now. We will move forward together, carrying the past in the rucksack of life.

When this is all over we will look to the future and step into our new world remembering what we have learned from the old. And those who are out of sight will remain in the hearts of those who have loved them, but happiness will be possible again.

Heather has been volunteering as a 'Listener' at Rennie Grove for three years.

Keeping in Touch by Sandy Kendall

Yes, we see the spring's unearthly green,
with the blue of sky and
white of clouds between.
And yes, we see their faces on the screen.

And we can hear the birdsong on the breeze,
and listen to the rustling of the trees.
And we can hear their voices on the ether
and the laughter that can do so much to ease.

But though we feel the softness of a petal,
touch is the heartache that the screen
can't settle. We cannot hug our loved ones
through the glass and metal.

*Sandy lives in Surrey. She is an artist and had her first novel
'A Dazzle of Poplars' as Alexandra Kendall published by
Cranthorpe Millner.*

Distanced by Heather Duffy

Let's FaceTime we say, knowing the technology will confuse
old faces peering from the corners of the screen,
lampshade taking precedence.
The weather, the doctor and news of empty days.
Words unspoken.
When will we see you?
When can you come?
When will this be over?

Senryu by Simon Tindale

The iPod broke down
at a service attended
by virtual friends.

Dim View by Hilary Feeney

After all we should have guessed
what might be happening
but chose to turn the other way instead.
So now we're walking on a thin black wire
where yesterday's fool Negligence
tears us apart: that same old shit again.

I'm on the other side of the glass
not where we should be.
Fingers smear an imprint
as we touch without the warmth of contact.
Your uncut nails bother me.
I should be there.

We're each other's ghosts
pressing against the pane.
You with your swoop of swallows' view
and mine a single bed with ornaments
from better days, waiting on a chest of drawers.

Leaning closer I breathe
half caught words of consolation
and maybe lies
until I blur, and through the mist
you see a stranger, start to turn away,
peripheral again.

I wonder, if I press a little harder
perhaps we'll feel the shattering?

Hailing from Yorkshire, Hilary has lived in the Tyne valley in Northumberland for over 40 years. She has four children and seven grandchildren (so far...).

Hands by Jane Edmonds

Now we cannot touch
I think of all the ways
our hands reach out to others:
we shake the hands of strangers,
pat the arms of friends,
hold the hands of lovers,
let grasp the birthing mother
and newborn's reflex grip,
console a tearful child,
hug a grieving spouse,
and stroke the softened hand
of someone at the end.

My Limbic Bear by Sarah Smith

I found you a place to rest, a hollow; silent and dark,
I am safe, you are safe.
The memory of you echoes execrably.
I am deafened, you are unmoved,
hibernating in isolation. Benign,
you are at peace; I am at peace.

Poked by a smell or the passing of time,
I unfold, you unfurl.
Padded paws of emotion are extended – you
cannot retract those claws.
You embrace, I brace.
Will they hug me or rip me apart
this time?

Sarah was a nurse for thirteen years. She lives in Nottingham where multitasking and going the whole day without stopping for the loo now help her to be a full-time mum, and to write. She uses writing to organize her thoughts, for expression and for herself.

Flesh and Glass by Virginia Betts

I imagine your real-life flesh
pixelated;
shattered into particles
smaller than dust;
filtered through airwaves,
and re-formed into your familiar face
to meet me, divided
by glass.

My fingertips touch
your hard, flat form,
tracing the valleys
and peaks
of your mapped-out features.
I could get lost in your landscape,
attempting to navigate
this severed connection.

What keeps us going
is knowing
that time will come
when the distance between us dissolves into flesh,
and hands, not voices, overlap;
and eyes, not screens, light up
to guide us back home.

Virginia runs a tuition company, Results Tutoring, in Ipswich, Suffolk. She has previously had non-fiction, poetry and short stories published in print and online. Her collection of short stories, 'The Camera Obscure' is to be published in 2021.

The Window Visit by Brian Kelly

You can have a window visit, the care home manager said;
only masks, no visors.
I went, I rang the bell.
A figure, masked and gowned, pushed the door ajar
then pointed at a blue plastic chair
lying in the porch, toppled by the wind,
like pandemic tumbleweed.
The same figure, this time inside,
rapped a window,
gestured towards the bewildered figure,
slumped in the stain-proof vinyl covered chair.
Twenty minutes visit – that's the rules!
Hi, Mum! – I waved – but no reaction.
I pulled the window open a little further.
No! You can't do that! Four inches – that's the rules!
So … I didn't speak, I shouted.
Family names; addresses; beloved pets;
battling through that fetid fog we know as Alzheimer's;
thicker by far than the man-made window.
I sang, played songs on my phone.
But nothing, until …
'Meet me in St Louis, Louis,
Meet me at the fair.
Don't tell me the lights are shining…'
And then – some lights did shine;
her eyes – became her own eyes.

214

She croaked my name – twice.
Trying to stand up, she pawed at the window
with frail filo fingers.
Her pane becoming our pain.
Time's up! I'm sorry – that's the rules!

Brian is 61, from Belfast and now lives in rural County Down, Northern Ireland. He worked in the NHS for 32 years and for 6 years in Queen's University, Belfast.

Senryu by Nick Hawkins

In a shed somewhere
someone sits alone and thinks
up conspiracies.

Nick lives in St Albans, Hertfordshire. 51-year-old father of two boys. Working from home most days. Now retired from Buckinghamshire New University. Refugee from the Smoke.

Balcony by Henry Magee

Sit with me now
in different rooms,
beside me
at a distance. Come
drink a glass of wine
with me onscreen
for old times' sake, it's good
for our stomachs too, I hear.
And do you like the view?
The sea is near,
a sparkling friend, it's
just beyond
my balcony.
We'll talk about the days
of traffic noise and
greeters' kisses, handshakes,
rounds of drinks:
life's hits and misses,
walk, or run
along the promenade;
the scent of food
from crowded restaurants,
bills footed, sounds
of children's fun.
Life was, if not always good,
at least proxemics, with
the audio unmuted.

And then the links
were broken.

Now there's greyness
just beyond
my balcony
and rain comes down,
(ain't life a bitch?),
but it will fill
the bowls I left there
for the birds to drink
and it will green
the land and
we'll get rich
from mining all that silver
from the lining
of the clouds.

Almuñécar

By kind permission of Helen Masterson. Henry was a retired health worker from Ireland and lived in Almuñécar, Spain. (28th October 1950-29th August 2020.)

A New App by Adrian Spalding

Following a recent virus attack, we strongly advise you to reset your world and install 2020v2.1. This update is more resilient and improved to deal with future security issues and bugs.

Install instructions:

A. Shutdown normal living for at least six weeks.
B. Begin restart. Please note this stage will be slow as the updated system is being installed.
C. Once the message 'a new anti-virus is installed' you can then resume life with 2020v2.1

In this important update we have added the following fixes:

1. Acquiring money is no longer the objective of living.
2. Good health and well-being are now the new objectives of living.
3. Local community will be the default setting.
4. The salary of workers should reflect their value to society.
5. Health and social care are no longer controlled politically.
6. Home and family are the new priority.
7. Workplaces are adjusted to be closer to your home.
8. Less commuting required (see item 7).
9. Less pollution (see item 8) creating better health (see item 2).
10. National defence is now enhanced to include threats to health.

Thank you for installing World 2020v2.1 into your life. We hope you see a marked improvement.

Since retiring Adrian has achieved his dream of becoming an author, with four published books to his credit and a fifth in the making. His most successful books are a series following the humorous escapades of 'The Reluctant Detective'. Originally from Croydon, Surrey he now lives in Kent. www.adrianspalding.co.uk

Aspirations by Peter Keeble

At the crucial meeting held on video
at which everything will be decided
all of us are boxed up eager to persuade
but flicker and fade around our edges
as our fake backgrounds invade.

There's Mike proud before the Taj Mahal
while Larry has the Bridge of Sighs
hiding where his washing dries.
Some play with craziness – Maggie
with her close-up multi-coloured clowns
but down-to-earth Constance is content
with the sweeping Sussex Downs.
Graham chose the Great Pyramid of Giza,
Suzie the Sydney Harbour Bridge
redolent of her fragile life right out there on the edge.

But you look out showing off no such fiction
fronting up before your spartan rustic kitchen.
Could it be this hides a true sensation
and you're out there orbiting the Pillars of Creation?

Virtually There by Geoff Buckingham

When this is all over, I'll treat you to a drink, or maybe even two.

Because we can celebrate the good times, and no longer be blue.

We'll visit a restaurant just made for me and you.

Rather than wait on our doorsteps for the man from Deliveroo!

Perhaps the things we once took for granted we will treasure and cherish.

And be so grateful that neither us, nor our families were among those to perish.

To attend a play in a theatre without wearing a mask.

To see each other's faces, is that too much to ask?

The everyday things we missed, we now want back, and fast!

And no longer need to recoil when a jogger runs past!

To go to dances and parties and make one hell of a din.

And at last go out more often than my recycling bin!

To see loved ones close up, instead of a socially distanced peek.

And for someone special, a firm kiss on the cheek!

And lastly a group hug with us all in the same room.

No more restricted to our laptops and meeting on Zoom!

Geoff hails from Sunbury-on-Thames, Surrey and is a published playwright as well as the current holder of The Spelthorne & Runnymede Best Writer and Most Prolific Writer Awards. He has five comedy plays with www.stagescripts.com.

It Might Never Have Happened
by Mike Chandler

After all, they were not neighbours, as such. The postman and his wife lived on one side of the street, the tiny, elderly lady, alone now after the recent loss of her husband, lived on the other side and several houses along the road. No. Not neighbours at all. But if the pandemic brought any good, it was the sudden sparking of what they called in the 1940s' 'Dunkirk Spirit.'

Suddenly people were aware of those who lived around them. Not just the immediate neighbours: the ones you chatted to while washing the car or cutting the lawn, but the older ones you might have seen wearily tugging shopping trolleys behind them, or sweeping their front path, or perhaps as a pale face glimpsed looking out a downstairs' window.

The pandemic changed that. Doors were knocked on, acquaintances made – at a socially safe distance – and if there was little else you could do, you could at least give reassurance to the lonely or the vulnerable that someone nearby cared.

The postman fetches shopping for her now, and probably does not realise he is bringing her hope, as well as food.

Mike is 66 and a former archivist and researcher for ITN News. He is happily retired with his wife Carol, who puts up with him disappearing for hours to sit in front of a computer to try his hand at writing. He is the author of the 'Loreli Potts' series currently available on Amazon Kindle, and he is now working on the next two books in the series.

Distance Dancing by Vicky Richards

I danced on the carpet,
watching the three-by-two-inch screen
balanced on a stack of folders.
Those were the best days,
laughing at the jokes coming from your tiny mouth,
copying the movements of your insect-sized body,
talking for hours after class:
the week's frustrations and American politics.

The carpet wrecked my ballet shoes.
Fixed them. Twice.
You got sick of talking to yourself,
and banging your head on the ceiling light.
Spending hours looking at guidelines,
trying to get us back in a studio.
I sent you memes,
checked in every day.

After eighteen weeks, we met face-to-face.
Stole secret moments:
I had missed your hugs and ruffling your hair.
Back in a studio, finally, people to talk to.
But it's not the same:
lips hidden behind cartoon characters;
two metres apart; the smell of Dettol everywhere;
no floor work … no lifts … no high fives at the end.

I'm weary, of the distance,
just me, at home, all week.
My one evening of dancing keeps me going,

our secret hug just about lasting me till the next class.
To be back in the pub, all of us laughing,
crammed together at the corner table,
sharing three packets of crisps …
That's the dream.

Vicky works as a freelance editor in a small village just outside of Cambridge. She has always had a passion for poetry, inherited from her grandmother, who would often recite verses from one poem or another. She has never published a poem, but has a whole collection saved up that she wrote as a child, so maybe one day she will publish some of them!

Dancing Amongst the Constellations
by Michelle Gunner

Clouds and rainbows for costumes,
I watch the dancers go
pirouetting around our planet
along the stars and the sun.
Earthbound no more, flying
propelled to the moon
leaping to undreamt heights.
Feet darting between Jupiter and Saturn,
arabesques stretching into infinity.
Feathers scattered in the universe
they dance, dance ecstatic,
an extravagant, extra-terrestrial ballet
in The Silence of Eternity.

First published in Michelle's collection 'Collages'/New Generation Publishing and available on Amazon.

A Time to Dance by Fiona Castle

There's a well-known verse in the Bible, telling us, 'There is a time for everything, a season for every activity under the sun'. (Ecclesiastes 3.1) What season of life are you in? I would love to be able to say that I'm in full flow as a professional dancer and singer. Not anymore. I have tried to remain as fit as possible, but can no longer dance and, as the saying goes – everything hurts and whatever doesn't hurt doesn't move.

We all have to cope with different seasons; some of them might be very difficult, painful or sad. I performed, with great enjoyment, in many pantomimes, shows and musicals. One highlight was taking over the part of Liesl in the original production of *The Sound of Music* in the West End. When I married I gave up my career as my husband was working much of the time in the United States. Life has not always been easy for me, but the beautiful poem 'What God has Promised' by Annie Johnson Flint has been an encouragement to me through many seasons of my life.

'God has not promised skies always blue,

Flower-strewn pathways all our lives through.'

One thing I have learned is that whatever my circumstances, I should make the most of the different seasons of my life, so that I don't look back with regrets, knowing that God is with me whatever happens.

Fiona was born on the Wirral, North West England; went to a school studying Dance and Theatre Arts from the age of nine. Since marriage she has lived mostly in Buckinghamshire.

Him by Claire Wilson

There will be a candy buffet for the grandkids. Bacon rolls and cucumber sandwiches for the grown-ups. His favourite scones. We've booked the golf club – the place it seemed like he'd spent half his life. There will be pictures on the walls: of our younger days before the kids came along. Holidays. Achievements. Laughter. Anything to make it easier for the kids. We've argued over a band or a DJ. But a member at the club said they'd take care of that. One less thing for me to worry about. 'As long as they play 'Stand by Me' by Ben E King,' I'd replied. Our song. Whenever it came on, whether we were in the kitchen making breakfast or in the middle of a department store, he would grab me and dance. I'd mock him for being silly as my heart swelled with love.

We'll do him proud in the way that we were robbed of back in April when our world ended. A send-off fitting for the man he was. The father. Grandfather.

The only thing that won't be there is the person I want to be there the most.

Him.

Claire is an aspiring crime writer from Falkirk, Scotland.

WINTER

'THE WINTER OF OUR DISCONTENT'

SHAKESPEARE'S 'RICHARD THE THIRD'

What Is Hard? by Jim Dening

A hard winter is forecast,
with infections and cold weather,
for us moderates and temperates;
and what is hard? A foot of snow
along our country track would be fun –
I could turn on the four by four
in the tough old pickup truck
and bring supplies up from the town.
But what is fun? We will not see
the chaps who sleep in cardboard boxes
along Church Street throwing snowballs.
We will not see the old people
who queue outside the surgery
and the chemist throwing snowballs.

I used to imagine starting again,
so to speak, waking, alone, in a field
or a forest, with nothing, naked,
trying to keep warm under twigs and leaves,
looking for abandoned rags to be able
to emerge on to a street – and then what?
to beg? to work? and to realize
that in hard times we may depend on others.

Working in the Townships by Khululwa Nkatshu

I'm trying to get myself together and try to hustle so I can be able to help at home since my mother stopped working as a domestic worker in June. So writing is irritating when you not gonna be focused on the subject and I have to say Covid-19 is annoying. It hasn't come with any positive news for me which I've been waiting for in a long time and thought 2020 would bear good fruit but nothing. So you will have to wait on me too for the good things. I don't feel like expressing myself since this whole topic is a bit depressing for me 'cause all I can think of is negative vibes for me.

But I know I did some good during this time in my community and need to work. Today I had the opportunity of donating 40 sanitary pads with contraceptive educational pamphlets, 80 fabric face masks to 40 young individuals in my community Masiphumelele whose homes were affected by the fire in December. These were given by donations from Noordhoek and FishHoek Community Action Network and Code Red Initiative. (2020)

I am thankful to everyone who continues to help me in making change in my community.

Khululwa's first language is Xhosa. She lives in the township Masiphumelele, Fish Hoek, Cape Town. She works voluntarily with young people helping them understand about sexual health and seeks paid work. She appeared in Jan Moran Neil's one-woman play 'A President in Waiting …' at the Desmond Tutu HIV Foundation Youth Centre, at the Gugu S'Thebe, Langa and Masambe Theatre, Baxter.

Aspirins and Austen by Patricia Sentinella

An elusive dream, a magic spell, golden dust falling from the sky, layering us with a healing balm or perhaps a less distant prospect when we shrug that we have had Covid-19 a couple of times this year, as casually as if we were brushing a fly from our water glass or talking about a mild dose of 'flu.

When I was younger, I was very susceptible to influenza, never thinking of it as a killing machine, though I must surely have heard of the 1918 devastation. Perhaps not, my general knowledge in those days was fairly non-existent, my head full of love and literature. I would take myself to bed with aspirin and Austen, pull the covers tight, sleep and read until I found after several days suddenly that I was ravenous for baked beans or scrambled egg and thick white toast.

In the winter of 1964, I caught 'flu three times in as many months.

After the third illness I felt so weak and unsteady that I was afraid to go outside, I would have welcomed a lockdown. Instead I managed a breathless, unsteady stagger downhill to my elderly Austrian GP, who had a passion for P G Wodehouse. He tried to convert me to his cause by posting sheets of badly copied extracts of Bertie's and Jeeves's adventures into my letter box. He was much better at curing my terrors with his generous doses of little white pills.

Perhaps there will be a pill one day, maybe large and difficult to swallow.

Here in Coronavirus Land 2020, I haven't left my cottage since March. I'm happy with the dietician telephone calls and they save me the tedious journey to the John Radcliffe with its traffic jams, stream-lined corridors and disapproving chairs.

Happy to let my hair grow unruly and have long, frequent telephone talks with my daughter.

In time everyone will put on masks and gloves to go out as naturally as taking an umbrella in the rain, measure distances to keep themselves safe and hope never to meet the person in their path carrying a loaded gun.

Born in London, Patricia has lived in a small village in South Oxfordshire for over 40 years. She taught creative writing to adults for many years, then discovered Creative Ink classes which helped her find form and direction for her own writing. Patricia's poetry collection: 'Dear John, Dear Anyone …' is published by Creative Ink and gave rise to the film 'Dear John, Dear Anyone …' with Patricia being one of the twelve finalists.

Winter Haiku by Maureen Bradley

World winter solstice.
We wait a while and wonder.
Wisteria wish.

Tunnels by George Bell

Because of medical reasons I have been confined to bed for eighteen months, only being allowed out of bed for two hours a day. I have never left my house in all this time. You can imagine, spending so much time on my own in my bedroom has affected my mental health. I have daily visits from the district nurse service. Several of the nurses noticed a change in my behaviour and reported this to my GP. As a result he has referred me to Mind. I had feelings of loneliness, felt that life was passing me by. I became an outsider looking in at life. I felt that some of those closest to me had abandoned me. Longstanding friendships I thought would never end seemed to melt away like snow upon the arrival of spring. Feelings of despair began to fill my days. It seemed to me that the light at the end of the tunnel had been turned off.

George is from Belfast and lives in Manchester. He has published 'Connie's Wars' a historical fiction set in Belfast and two volumes of 'Adventures in Angel-Wing Forest: Imogen and Little George'.

The Great Unlocked by Simon Tindale

Tonight we count the clock down.
The builder is a block down.
The banker is a stock down.
The boxer is a knock down.

The jeweller is a rock down.
The dresser is a frock down.
The vicar is a flock down.
The student is a mock down.

The shoe shop is a sock down.
The sweet shop is a choc down.
The gun store is a Glock down.
The spaceship is a Spock down.

And so the tickers tock down.
It's time to put the wok down
and write another crock down
about a life in lockdown.

Unlocking Lockdown by Jennifer Morais

Lockdown
inside I hide
invisible threats

time
passes, pauses –
yet, more time is found

less travel
less doing
less choices

more being ...
inside your home
inside your mind

making history
new habits
new yearnings

the masks
muffled sounds
hidden smiles
distant ... kind eyes

community spirit
successful science
feelings of hope

awaiting the day...

lockdown is unlocked.

Long sentence. (*Last line added by Editor.*)

London-born with Colombian and Portuguese roots, Jennifer lives in High Wycombe, Buckinghamshire with her partner. She was made redundant from her Internal Communications role with a charity during the pandemic and has since become a Zumba fitness instructor.

Lockdown Open by John Ling

Walking us from wing to wing,
he asks us to imagine each
space filled with human life.
Here they meet to chat, he says,
watch the match, play pool,
cook, paint, make things.
Each exit and entrance we
pause while he jangles keys
swinging from his heavy belt,
outer door and inner door,
great clanging iron grilles
echo harshly down the wing,
flashes ID, waits for lights,
looks at cameras, speaks to mikes.
In each empty wing, in rows
along the walls, thick green doors
face away from us, with one
tiny eye hole, handleless,
only key holes. And behind
every door, he does not say,
a man sits, we imagine,
lies, stands, stretches, paces,
silent, anxious, angry, bored,
bored, bored, bored, tired of
wasting, wasting, waiting, willing
that door to be opened wide.

Closed Doors by Tony Domaille

I don't open the door to that room anymore. There are flies. I can hear them if I get close. I know I need to call someone about it; and I will when this is all over, but not now. You can't have people in your house. The government ministers keep saying so in the daily briefing. Not until the virus has gone.

But when they do come, I'll have showed them. Doctors, social workers; what do they know? They think I can't cope on my own, but it's been three months now and I've got by without any help at all. We lived through the rationing years, so I know how to make things last. Powdered milk is the secret.

It's true, I wish my George was still alive, and then at least I'd have someone to talk to. But you just make do, don't you? The only thing I haven't managed is changing the light bulbs. I can't use the step ladder, not with my legs. It'll have to wait until you're allowed to have someone in your house. Then they can fix that for me, take George's body, and get rid of the flies.

In a past life Tony was a police officer, working on child abuse cases, and sadly the lockdown made him wonder about hidden children. He lives in South Gloucestershire and primarily writes for the stage. He has a number of award-winning plays published by Lazy Bee Scripts.

Get a Handle on It by Elizabeth Wilson

When all this is over, my neighbours probably want to replace their door handle. I spotted its relocation when I left for a walk. Nondescript chrome, the sort you get in a hotel or almost-trendy apartment block for 'young professionals'. It lay on the hot-pink doormat, leaving a gaping hole above the keyhole.

Last winter I answered a frantic knocking in the late evening. The man of the house needed a screwdriver – or rather, his friend who didn't have the wide, red-rimmed eyes of a panicking stoner, needed the screwdriver – to take off the handle and manually unlock the stuck catch. I thought they'd fixed it. Maybe their landlord isn't prompt at repairs.

Our door handle looks the same. I don't trust it now. Each time I leave, I waggle it. Test it. Since all this began, my natural shyness has mutated into an anxious cloud that clings to me when I leave the house. The threat of the door handle is just something new to add to the paranoia.

It catches in the fold of my sleeve when I hurry home, jerking me back outside. Politely reminding that it can separate me from home.

Elizabeth lives in York, partly because she loves medieval history. She occasionally blogs on Folklore and Pop Culture at <u>*www.scranshums.com*</u>

The Closed Door by Angela Andrews

She looks like my mother,
her hair's still the same,
and just once she looked up
at the sound of my name.

I tell her stories
of our homes by the sea;
remind her of pranks
by my brother and me.

We walk in the garden,
take in the fresh air;
slow steps of resistance
no companionship there.

She thinks we have met
but not quite sure when;
a carer, a doctor
maybe an old friend.

She's scared and confused
behind still lovely eyes;
no chance, cruel thief
to say our goodbyes.

I wish I could go in
through the door to her mind,
unravel confusion
leave anguish behind.

I Wish You Were Closer by Tony Domaille

'I wish you were closer,' she said.

She knew I couldn't be. Maybe when the pandemic was over, but for now this was the best we could do. I put my palm to the Perspex screen between us and watched her raise her own frail, wrinkled hand to meet mine. Close, but still a world away. Then she launched into her stories. Back in time when I did things that made her laugh or cry or proud, and her eyes lit up at her memories. I had groomed the dog with garden shears. I had flooded the bathroom playing submarines. I had won school prizes, been kind, had the finest wedding day she had ever known, and been the best son a mother could ever wish for.

'You've always been a lovely boy,' she said, putting her palm to the screen again.

I mirrored her hand. 'You're lovely yourself.'

And then the care worker was there behind her, tapping at his watch and mouthing that it was time I was leaving. As I signed myself out, the care home manager must have read my mind, because she said, 'Dementia isn't always a curse, you know. Mary thinks you're her son'.

The Heart of the Home by Kathryn Prior

Home is where the heart is. Where memories are created. Where muddy football boots and shoes tumble over each other, cluttering up the hallway. Aromas of Sunday roast waft round the kitchen; the heart of the home exuding laughter and noise. Plates piled high with cabbage, carrots, parsnips and peas, thick juicy, succulent slices of roast beef and Yorkshire pudding, smothered in horseradish sauce, with lashings of gravy. Comforting, delicious, familiar. Wine flows; conversation is noisy; laughter, debating, arguing. A cacophony of voices, vying to be heard.

Apple pie follows, bursting with fresh apples, lovingly picked from the tree in the garden they all climbed when they were small. The tree still has the scars, as do their knees. The floorboards creak from the memories of Sunday lunch. Silence creeps out from every corner, swirling memories through the air. Home is where the heart is. But where is the heart now?

She walks through the newly decorated hall for one last time. Closing the door behind her. The SOLD sign swaying in the wind, knocking into the apple tree. She gets in her car to drive to visit her mum, 'The Heart', in the nursing home down the road.

Kathryn was part of the marketing team for 'Rhyme & Reason' in the 1990s.

Waiting ... by Jessica Cox

My mum is lying in the intensive care unit. I have just said goodbye to her over FaceTime. I am not allowed to see my mum as she lay dying because despite having had the vaccine, visitors are not allowed in.

Covid has fucked my mum up. She was a fun-loving, independent woman a year ago. She had a better social life than anyone I know. Fit and healthy with friends, she was full of vitality. Covid has stripped her of her essence. She has lived in confinement. Afraid of catching this disease with an approximate 95% survival rate* in case she dies of it. Well she is dying. Not of Covid. Of kidney failure. She has languished in her home. Having visits at the window from her children. Children she has been too afraid to allow in. Too afraid to cuddle. Because we have to follow 'the rules' don't we – or we will die? She stopped caring. Caring for herself. Deteriorating before my eyes. Not knowing how to help her. She had given up you see. Living in the dark. But not living. We aren't allowed to live in case we pass on Covid. And now she is dying. A real irony there. And still I can't hold her hand. I can't hold her close. I can't hear her voice. I can't tell her how much I love her as she drifts into her final sleep. I'm not allowed in. And I am angry. So very fucking angry. My mum who nurtured and cared for me deserves more than this. More than a year of nothing. Only to die anyway. Alone. With strangers. While I sit here.

Waiting for the phone call.

Mother's Day 2021

In the absence of underlying health conditions

Jessica has performed in five of Creative Ink's plays and films. She runs the Spotlight Drama School for youngsters. She is a qualified criminal psychologist.

Leaving ... by Tony Domaille

When this is all over, I'll leave. Even if my plan works, I can't stay. How can I stay when Mum knows he comes to my room every night? When she knows what he does? I don't know why she loves him more than me. But it's all the things that are wrong with him that gave me my plan. He's obese. He's diabetic. I know he takes tablets for high blood pressure and high cholesterol. I know he's at risk.

They haven't noticed my cough. They don't know I have a temperature and I can't taste anything. I really don't feel too terrible, but I know I've got the virus, and I'm going to use it. When he comes to my room tonight, I won't turn away from his kiss. Tonight, I'll give him everything he wants ... and something he doesn't.

Once he has the virus, I suppose he'll give it to Mum, and I don't know how I feel about that. Maybe they'll both be like me and just feel a bit rough, but I want him to die. Yes, once this is all over, I'll leave. My life is out there when the world opens up again.

Mum Guilt by Hannah Vessey

While out walking, the sight of daffodils made me cry, tears of relief, I think. They signified to me the end of a long and lonely winter. I have found this lockdown intensely hard, and I have felt very guilty for finding it so hard. It should be easy to stay at home, with my lovely family, where we are comfortable and safe. I have easily been able to keep in contact with family and friends but still, I have been down and short-tempered with my partner and small children.

In fact, I've felt guilty for lots of things; for not doing enough home schooling, for not having enough fun with my children or neglecting them to get housework done, gaining weight, not giving enough energy to my job in social care. It's been tough trying to keep all these plates spinning and experiencing this constant, nagging feeling that I am not quite doing enough.

I work for a charity which provides support, and educational and social opportunities for people with learning disabilities: a group of people for whom the pandemic has been, for some, particularly isolating, confusing and frightening. I am continually impressed by the resilience and determination of these people I 'support' because, truth be told, they have helped me through the weeks and months as much as I have them.

Hannah, Buckinghamshire. Mum of two under-fives and part-time support worker.

Stormed by Sarah Robin

Dark grey skies eliminate the light and a mighty rumble of thunder echoes violently within my head. As the negativity of each day crashes down on me with the force of freak hailstorms, treacherous rainfall batters down on my thoughts leaving me unable to concentrate. Fear of death and destruction keeps me under cover; not venturing outside because it's unsafe. Gale-force winds knock my emotions unbalanced, spending day after day lying in my bed hiding away from what's happening in the world. I'm alone but I'm protected and warm. Sacrificing human interaction with friends and family so as not to be contaminated.

There's nothing else to do than to be alone with my thoughts and wait.

Sarah is a new writer from Bolton, North West England. She has already had several short stories published in anthologies and is a poetry competition winner. She was furloughed and then made redundant.

The Virus (after Thomas Gray) by Janet Rogers

The curfew tolls the knell of parting day.
Ghost towns emerge from busy city life
as to our homes we trace our weary way
and leave the world to darkness and to strife.

Now fades the life that once we knew so well
and all the air a disconnection holds.
No touch, no sound 'cept that of clanging bell.
It tolls the stench of death which now unfolds.

And from our prison cell we watch and wait,
crouched in hushed fear yet never to complain
while others suffer breathless for their fate;
there is no cure to take away the pain.

The virus creeps into our very soul,
death slicing through this green and pleasant land.
It picks at random, takes its rotten toll,
grasps, grabs and squashes like a giant's hand.

It points a finger, traps its victim square,
works quickly and with fever lays them low.
Keeps them bound and tied down in its lair
before it strikes the final, fatal blow.

We've had our brush with death, it was not fair
to take so many unsuspecting folk
and treat them with such lack of human care.
We cry for them, we mourn, it was no joke.

Janet lives by the sea at East Preston on the Sussex coast. She has won several national travel writing competitions and had her work published in the national press. She is a 'Writing Magazine' contributor.

Natural Remedy by Alwyn Gornall

We pause,

to let the virus pass,
and in that window
of opportunity the
natural world breathes
a sigh of relief.

It begins to heal itself.

Alwyn has been published in 'On Writing', 'Another North', 'Dreich' and 'Highland Park Poetry'. Nowadays he concentrates on developing his poetry, writing children's fiction, staying out of trouble and supporting the writing community in Newcastle, North East England.

In the Long Run by Peter Poole

When Covid's gone, raise a cheer! But what's so new?
We'll muddle on – day by day – that's me and you.
The noisy throng, on the march, *they'll* make a do.
Things went wrong! Rights are rights! And who to sue?

Give us a rest. For goodness sake! Just let it go.
We took the test, did our bit – what's there to know?
We lost some friends, think on that – a crushing blow.
Can't make amends; swallow hard, life's bitter flow.

And when we're through, gather strength. We must prepare:
we'll build anew, cut no cost, with endless care.
But what's the fright we now face? A solar flare?
Big meteorite? Another disease, so rare?

We'll never know. When it hits us, it'll be too late.
Which volcano, spewing lava, will seal our fate?
Just seek your fun, live this life, but keep your head ...
in the long run, sad truth is: we'll all be dead.
March 2021

Peter is retired and living on a farm in Northumberland, where day-to-day life seems hardly to have been touched by Covid, though he writes he realizes that is definitely not true of other places.

Making My Mark by Ben Crowden

I went out for a walk today,
around the town and down the docks,
but found I had nothing to say
amidst the ships and shut up shops.
I could not seem to find the words;
all my attempts to rhyme just died.
All of my efforts for the birds,
like ice-cream at the harbour side,
I could not put my pen to pad without it sounding insincere,
like something from an awful ad
that's selling loans or real ale beer.
But sat upon a bench alone I looked up to the hills and spied
the pretty pastel painted homes;
those vulnerable still stuck inside
and thought how lucky I have been
to spend this time with someone dear
when there are those who have not seen
a friendly face at all this year.
So while lockdown has been all right
for those in better health like me
I'm glad there's now an end in sight
for those who haven't felt so free.
Thus I came back and in my hall,
I got some use out of my pen; marking the days until we all
can hold all those we love again.

*Ben is a writer and performer from Beaconsfield,
Buckinghamshire, currently based in Bristol. He has spent the last
five years designing and running escape rooms. He performed in
Creative Ink's play 'The Deadly Factor'.*

My Cancer Journey During Covid by Robin Miller

The 5th of September 2019 will forever be etched in my heart: a day that everything was turned upside down. A doctor trying to tell you with compassion that you have cancer. Is this really happening to me was my first thought. Then how bad is it came out of my mouth. Bad was an answer I didn't want to hear. Firstly an operation, then chemotherapy treatment for a year. Everyone is different. It depends on how you fight the fight, he said. You seem fit and you're relatively young.

I was a deflated soul coming out of the treatment room. My first appointment for the cancer clinic dropped on the hall floor. Opening the lift door to the cancer centre, how did I get here I was asking myself. Hearing your name called and sitting down with your consultant for the first time was an experience hopefully I will not have to do again. 'Robert your cancer has spread.' This guy wasn't sugarcoating anything. He looked worried which didn't help. This can go either way.

So it began, having a tube inserted into your arm to enable the nurses to administer the chemotherapy. A year of treatment and bloods, in between having a scan lying on a scanner and being pumped up with a dye. Man, you can feel this charging through your veins.

I was very lucky to get through it reasonably smoothly. I'm definitely amazed by the care and compassion I was shown by all the nurses and doctors on my journey to cancer-free. Without them superstars I would not be here. I can't express or repay my gratitude and thanks to them all. Hopefully I will live to a 100 and stun everyone.

Robin lives in Bangor, Northern Ireland.

Still Standing by Busisiwe Dlongwana Lolo

I'm Busisiwe Lolo staying in Cape Town, with my two kids: Joy and Tutu and my husband. The pandemic really affected us, emotionally, financially. I'm the business woman (selling Tupperware products and clothing) and it was so hard for me because my customers did not have money to pay me, or the money to buy. Most of them were retrenched* from work.

As for my husband who is working in film industry as a freelance grip, it became worse because he has to stay at home with no income for about six months and we have bills to pay. We have to pay bond,** the car, policies and food. It was so hard. We were forced to go stay in Eastern Cape for about three months because life there is not as expensive as the one in Cape Town. But we thank God that we still standing.

The saddest part of it, I lost three of my best friends: one in April, one in June and one in December 2020 and all three because of this Covid.

It was a terrible experience because we living in fear.

*Made redundant, ** Mortgage.

Busisiwe's first language is Xhosa. She is originally from Cofimvaba in the Eastern Cape. She now lives in Eerste Rivier, Western Cape. She has completed a First Aid Course and Home Base Care.

Upward and Onward by Sam Harvey

To represent Wales's Disability Cricket Team at Lord's famous cricket ground when I was nineteen was a wonderful experience and to be there with my friends made it all the better. It felt awesome to be on the pitch and winning was the best feeling ever. I felt so proud being presented with my medal. It's proof that being disabled shouldn't be a barrier or hold you back as I also represented Wales in athletics, throwing the club when I was seventeen.

Since the pandemic started last March my world has gotten very much smaller. I really miss being able to play disability sport which is an essential part of my social interaction and so beneficial to keeping me fit and healthy. I also miss all the concerts and theatre shows and cinema visits and being able to visit places of interest but mostly I miss seeing my friends. I have also gained a great deal during the pandemic as well: by discovering lots of walks in the countryside near to where I live and getting close to nature which is accessible in my wheelchair. I've met many local people along the way who I now class as friends. I loved learning to bake and being resourceful in thinking of new things to try. Social media has also been important to keep in touch with the outside world. I have kept my spirits up and take one day at a time and know that life will get back to normal in the not too distant future.

Sam is 31 and from Cardiff, South Wales. He was born with Cerebral Palsy and a heart condition.

The Rainbow by Lizzie Axtell

I think of the rainbow colours as emotions that we feel.
As Covid-19 invades us, the experience surreal.
Red, fear of attack, a tyrant in our midst.
Orange, anxiety of the unknown, questions, the growing list.
Yellow, a sunny disposition, our true colour will keep
shining through.
Green, stoicism and calmness to carry on, regardless how
difficult for me and you.
Blue, despair at all lives lost, the enormity of this disease.
Indigo, reflection, taking stock of the progress we have
achieved.
Violet, hope for the future when the pandemic of the world
subsides.
The rainbow etched in history as the poignant symbol of our
time.

*Lizzie is a 68-year-old living in Aston Clinton,
Buckinghamshire with her husband and dog; enjoying writing
stories and poems for the early years and poems for family and
friends; with the lockdown inspiring stories for her youngest
grandson.*

Starting Over by Charlotte Booth

I hope the world will be a better place: less pollution, more interaction and a greater appreciation of the small things in life. But we are only human. When this is all over we will revert to normal in an unrecognizable world. Thousands of businesses, bars and shops will be gone for good. The dying High Street will be dead and buried. Struggling pubs will have pulled their last pints. But we will adapt. When this is all over we will all switch off Zoom and our smart phones. We will meet people in the flesh and appreciate their company. Really?

When this is all over, things we craved whilst in lockdown, we learned to live without. How essential is a monthly haircut? Are my nails stronger without gel polish or acrylic nails? Do we need to eat out every week? Habits only take twenty-one days to change.

When this is all over we will need to once more get used to being in close proximity with people. We will need to unlearn the fear that the outside and other people are dangerous. When this is all over, we'll start again.

Charlotte lives in Wiltshire and is a professional copywriter and writer of non-fiction books – mostly about Egypt. 'History of the Undead' by Pen and Sword is to be published this year.

Sonnet to Post Covid? by Jonathan Dancer

How this little ball of protein felled us,
with all our misplaced sense of self-import.
Those who saw it tried so hard to tell us
we could not be as powerful as we thought.
Empty bubbles we believed would save us
burst coldly in dark streaks of acid rain.
Pouring down, remorseless hard and fearless,
our self-inflated hubris seared in pain.
Finding wholesome things now we're unfettered,
and wondering what this means whilst we reflect.
We can only hope that something better
emerges from the ash and interjects
to replace the structures we were building,
lighting fires of love with brand new kindling.

Jonathan lives in Sussex and is a new author. He hopes to publish the first book in his new trilogy shortly. For more information, please visit www.jmdancerauthor.com He grew up in Penn and wrote this sonnet for his mother Pat Dancer after her passing in 2019. Pat was a first 'Rhyme & Reason' editor in 1992.

Better Stuff Ahead by Pam Lish

We'll all be older, if not wiser. Priorities will change and life will never be the same again. Maybe our new-found sense of community will bring us closer together. A sobering thought! Can the wartime-style camaraderie that has seen neighbours helping neighbours and young helping old set a precedent for the future? Will the drive to grow and cook our own produce survive once we have less time on our hands?

If there was ever a time for change, this is it. Future generations depend on what happens next. This is a golden opportunity to save our planet and make it a cleaner and safer place for children to grow up in. Already there are changes afoot. The battle against climate change and excessive consumerism has already been given a boost by this global pandemic. When this is all over we can only hope that we are able to meet the challenges left in its wake and build a better world.

Pam is over 70 and, for several years, has been a member of a delightful U3A writers' circle.

Behaving by Jackie Fuell

When on March 23rd 2020 Boris told us to stay indoors I knew our lives and the way we were would never be the same for a very long time. I thought I would keep a diary. Well after two weeks I had written, 'A nothing day' and my highlight was the daily bulletin from Downing Street. I thought I must make these days count. I wrote letters to friends and made phone calls. I sorted my clothes and cupboards then realized no charity shops were open so I have a very full car boot. I made my first Christmas cake. I bought a lot of fashion masks: all colours and styles but they used to steam up my glasses. The only ones that didn't were the regular 'use once' ones. You could put your tongue out or smile – nobody would know under that mask.

I have had my first jab and now people are saying to each other which jab have you had. I have watched funerals of friends online. I cannot see us getting back to normal. I know I shall never take anything for granted and I am very grateful I have survived so far. I will continue to listen to the powers that be and behave myself and await my second jab to hopefully have freedom and will continue wearing my mask – part of my make up now.

Jackie, aged 77, lives in Woodside, London, very married with children, grandchildren and great grandchildren and she writes that she has had lived a full and happy life. So far.

Oh Frabjous Day! by Jeff Galatin

Unlikely heroes they might be
but an encounter with these three:
Jabbatwork, Banderscratch and Jabjab Bird
will save many lives if true to their word.

There's a gyre and gimble in the air.
No slithy toves to spread despair.
With vaccine-filled vorpal syringe in hand,
victory is in sight for this mighty band.

After a deft and quick snicker-snack
the precious liquid goes on the attack.
A mimsy feeling floods my whole being.
Oh frabjous day – at last Covid's fleeing?

Jeff is a volunteer in the Rennie Grove Bookshop in Princes Risborough, Buckinghamshire.

One Day by Toni Mannell

One day we will look back upon this:
that day when we can again hug and kiss
when we can stand in line to check out our food
with a smile and a word, rather than a tense nod and
mood.

With distancing eased
we'll be cautiously pleased
back to a new norm
without that worry worm
churning in our minds
making sleep hard to find.

Days without masks is all we ask.
One day, one fine day
this pandemic will go away.

Toni is almost 60 and has been writing articles, short stories and poetry as long as she can remember. She retired five years ago to look after her disabled dog, who sadly she lost in January 2020. She enjoys daily walks with her black Labrador and camera. From Fareham, Hampshire.

A Modern Fable by Rodney J Mazinter

The ant works hard all summer long, building his house and gathering food for the winter.

The grasshopper laughs, dances and plays the summer away. Comes winter, the shivering grasshopper demands to know why the ant should be allowed to be warm and well fed while he is cold and starving. The country's newspapers show pictures of the grasshopper outside while the ant is warm at home with a food-laden table.

How can this be, that among wealth the grasshopper is allowed to suffer so? Activists with banners flying, chant, 'Green Lives Matter', 'Occupy the Anthill'. They blame Apartheid, Donald Trump, Colonialism, and Israel for the grasshopper's plight. The ant's home is confiscated by the government and given to the grasshopper.

We see the grasshopper and his free-loading friends finishing the last of the ant's food while his house that he cannot afford to maintain, crumbles around him. The house, now abandoned, is taken over by a gang of spiders who terrorize the once prosperous neighborhood.

Rodney is a regular writer to newspapers, online journals, and has had poems published in a number of magazines and anthologies in South Africa. He has also published a novel with a second in the process of being written, is creating a travel series of CDs, and co-written a book on the Rugby World Cup.

Journey by Louis Di Bianco

All pain comes from resistance. I first heard that statement circa 2010. It hooked my mind. Simple and profound. I understood the words. But I didn't truly *know* their meaning. Knowing is experiential, not intellectual. It happens at a cellular level. It disrupts and transforms.

When Covid-19 upended the world in March 2020, I wanted to *know* what it meant. My mind spun four narratives, one for each quarter since March 2020. All but one were wrong.

The first was my *Hoax Story*. The pandemic was fake. A global ruse created by and for the benefit of an elite cabal.

Then came the *Pity Story* that aroused my anger. It gave me license to complain, rant, blame, and brood. All forms of resistance that nurture, intensify, and justify pain.

Next, the *Reluctant Acceptance Story*. I began to enjoy silence. Loneliness slowly morphed into solitude. I stopped drinking alcohol. I was moving, with strong resistance, toward Being instead of Doing.

Today, I'm living my *Gratitude Story*. I experience it beyond my mind. I'm grateful for my five senses, a blooming amaryllis, a black cat's meow, a stranger's smile. Things I've always had.

Joy comes from letting go.

Louis is an international stage and screen actor and teacher. He was born in New York City and lives in Toronto, Canada. He publishes a video on acting for the camera every Friday on his YouTube channel, 'Screen Acting Success'.

The Scent of the Moon by John-Christopher Johnson

I want to walk, run
and jump. Skim over

a pond's surface like
one of The Dambusters's

bouncing bombs, ride
on wings of dragonflies,

drift spore-like,
airborne and contented,

feel the sap in flowers
and my own blood rising,

shake hands with the sun,
lay my head on pillows

of green or tawny moss.
I'll worship ducks

and swans as they've
always glided serenely,

learn lessons from
their tranquility. Throw

stones like boomerangs
and know they'll return.

Smell the scent of the moon
trailing across mountains.

I'll watch my own rejuvenation,
rapidly unfurling like a petal

blessed with affection.

*Chris has been contributing to such magazines as 'Acumen',
'Agenda', 'Interpreter's House', 'London Grip', 'Sentinel',' Orbis'.
Originally born in Bradford, West Yorkshire he now lives in
Reading, Berkshire.*

A Christmas Gift by Pat Aylett

What do you wish for this Christmas?
What will be under the tree?
Will there be lots of surprises?
What are you hoping to see?

This Christmas will be like no other –
nothing we've coped with before.
We're facing an uncertain future.
I wonder what might be in store?

I don't want the usual presents,
no gift-wrapped surprises for me.
No flowers or perfume or chocolates,
that's not what I'm hoping to see.

I'd like something really quite tiny,
a gift that I've not had before –
a vial of a vaccine to save us,
there's nothing I'm longing for more.

A vaccine to see off the virus
and save me before I'm too old.
A vaccine to make life worth living,
a gift that's more priceless than gold.

December 2020

Pat lives in Stoke Mandeville, Buckinghamshire. She has been a client at Aston Hearing, Amersham for about twelve years and since the beginning of lockdown in March 2020 she has had a regular poetry slot in their monthly newsletters.

For You by John-Christopher Johnson

I bring you gold, frankincense
and myrrh wrapped

in the first Christmas paper.
No guiding star

led me to this choice.
I've used two layers

of sellotape so don't feel
in the need to hurry.

Choose any of them you
like. But before you do,

listen to the sound inside,
hold my gift up to both

your ears. Those lovely
octaves come from my

own chirruping heart.

Crafty Fundraising by Three Fundraisers: Ann Turley, Annie Bennett and Sue Lynch

By Ann Turley

A December day. A Christmas stall.
Wondrous gifts for one and all.
An army of helpers to help at the fair,
raising money for Rennie Grove Hospice Care.
Marmalade, jams and chutneys too,
a tasty treat just for you.
Christmas decorations made from rags,
wreaths, spectacle cases and lavender bags.
Beautiful cushions and table mats,
served by ladies in festive hats.
There was pottery, wood turning, plates and flowers,
displayed on gingham cloths over cardboard towers.
Thousands of pounds were raised that day,
as happy customers went on their way.

Ann has been a member of the Beaconsfield Fundraising Group since 1994 and has had fun raising money for this wonderful charity.

And by Annie Bennett

On a chilly afternoon in December a group of ladies from the Beaconsfield Fundraising Group came to my home to price and sort a wonderful variety of items that had been made by the exceptionally talented members of the committee. I am not one of the exceptionally talented members of the committee! It was my task to wrap, decorate and present these items for sale. Having been cut off from everyone due to the restrictions, it was a positive joy to be working together again for our much-loved Rennie Grove Hospice.

RGHC has been an enormous part of Annie's life for the past 28 years. The Beaconsfield Fundraising Group is not just a committee but a group of close friends with a single aim.

And by Sue Lynch

Racking our brains – How can we raise cash for our beloved charity?

Enterprising – Let's get crafting, making and cooking!

Never-ending list of amazing ideas from so many willing lovely ladies.

No places to be or people to see in lockdown!

Incredible amount of precious time on our hands put to great use.

Enthusiasm by the bucket load. A real sense of a community venture.

Golf Club – The perfect venue for our socially distanced craft fair and chosen Charity of the Year for Beaconsfield Captains.

Raised our spirits as well as cash. Everyone enjoyed the festive atmosphere.

Oh, my goodness – Just lucky with the date! A few days before December lockdown.

Very Successful – Beautiful things for sale. We raised over £3 K fantastic.

Everyone involved was so generous with their time, effort and materials to make this possible. Thank you

When Sue received a handwritten letter of thanks for her donation to the charity more than twenty years ago it was the catalyst for her becoming a fundraiser for Rennie Grove. She has been richly rewarded by the wonderful friendships and fun times to help an amazing local charity very close to her heart.

Our Legacy for the Future by Hazel Bendon
Senior Community Fundraiser
at the Rennie Grove Hospice Care

When lockdown happened in March 2020, fundraising at the charity ground to a halt. All events were cancelled and shops closed. I thought what on earth are we going to do now and how can we continue to fundraise!

Shortly after in April, I went on furlough whilst a reduced fundraising team continued to fathom what action was needed to raise funds. It was strange, as I felt in limbo being at home and had no idea of what the future would look like and just like everyone else was disbelieving what was happening.

Thank goodness in May I was back in work and eager like the rest of the team to present new ideas. We need to raise funds which provide specialist nursing care and support to adults and children with a life limiting illness.

Little did I know Zoom, Teams, Facebook and YouTube would become a vital part of our everyday lives and the word we are all so familiar with now 'virtual' is becoming our fundraising success!

For my colleagues and me, it has been a challenge to raise funds in these times but we have learnt so much so quickly and it has changed the way we think and fundraise. We have widened our fundraising horizons which is a legacy for the future and mined something fruitful in such difficult times.

Hazel worked in London for some 30+ years in the corporate sector when suddenly her husband became ill with cancer and she felt it was time to work closer to home in Milton Keynes, Buckinghamshire. Her husband is fine now and is in remission.

She decided to evaluate her work/life balance and wanted to do something that was worthwhile and helped the local community, so she chose a charity she was passionate about and became a community fundraiser, which she has loved doing over the past eight years.

Twenty by Maureen Bradley

2020: was the year full of promise, not what was expected but gave us plenty.
2021: slowly picking up the pieces and re-joining them again one by one.
2022: should be the year with hindsight help, we can press play for life anew.

Moving Tales by Angela Neve

'Cornwall is a Duchy, a proud Celtic nation. Cornwall is my home. Kernow Vys Byken!'

Our family home is almost sold. Time to move on. We don't want to lose it but the fate of our north coast haven is sealed. Developers are prowling, devouring and hungry for the land ... but how we will miss our view. Ever changing seascape, sunsets that envelop you as if transported to another planet.

Scanning the market and consuming the detail of housing schemes, a bleak picture is emerging. Cornwall is not the picture perfect place of media hype. Incomes are well below the national average, employment scarce and often seasonal. Cornwall was designated the second poorest EU region in recent years. Social problems bring challenges: angry, disaffected people. Queuing for my first AZ vaccination, a passer-by screamed at us over 65s. 'I hope you all die.' Curses echoing down the empty street. No home is truly affordable and many are losing hope. I'm poised for flight to my rented bolt hole: no homes left to buy.

When this is all over I will join the queue of re-locators. Brand 'Cornwall' ... windy lanes with a glimpse of the sea, smugglers' coves and of course cream teas. If you can get there for all the people and traffic.

Angela is 67, a retired widow having raised her family in a stunning north coast location overlooking the Atlantic and has decided to leave the family home of three decades. She writes that little did she know what a crazy, frenetic market she would be attempting to navigate during this time of Covid re-location panic.

New Year Letter by Patricia Sentinella

We shop in the rain
for potatoes and red wine;
you split logs
while I contemplate the muddy track
that takes us deep into January
bump by bump.

We lean on the kitchen stove
breathing spiced smoke.
Glowing clear as cornelian
in your bright shirt
you spread out for me
red carpet of welcome.

Wintering in such warmth,
I have not forgotten the cold.
Forebodings of frost finger the glass
in the darkness before dawn;
chill messages creep early
through the letter-box.

In this windy country,
heat is hard won
and not continuous.
Your bus leaves in the half light.
I remain to arrange words like kindling
on the creased page.

First published in Patricia's collection 'Dear John, Dear Anyone…'/Creative Ink Publishing.

Missing by Jennifer Sherry

When this is all over
and there is not a daily tolling of death,
and we are not fearful of neighbours on the narrow footpath
or worried that an ever so slight
tickle in the throat is a first foreboding sign,

will we look back in wonder
on quiet days when
children rode bicycles unburdened by traffic
and people clapped with strangers and
chatted in long supermarket queues?

Will we miss the ease of morning free
from the pull of the commute,
when we turned our homes into nests with leftover Christmas
lights
and the smell of banana bread,
and the smiling face of a friend on a screen
was celebrated with fresh clothes and a glass of wine?

When this is all over
and we tally the cost,
will we ask ourselves how we coped
with the jagged tug of missing
the feel of another's hand in ours,
or a loved one in our arms?

Will we know why we were spared
when so many were lost?

Jennifer is originally from Canada and has been living here in the UK for eleven years. She currently lives in Gerrards Cross, Buckinghamshire and was one of the twelve finalists in Creative Ink's 'Dear John, Dear Anyone ...' film, 2012.

Walking for Health – January 2021 by Sue Johnson

We walk every day providing it's not pissing with rain.
We walk from our house along the January roads
because the fields we walked in summer are like
quagmires or paddy fields.

We see cyclists and dog walkers,
notice signs of spring in cottage gardens.
There are houses where the Christmas tree
still stands a month after Christmas Day.

This year, people are holding tight to fairy lights.
There is talk of worsening mental health.
We walk to give structure to our days, to take away
the fear of what the future holds.

Friends by Margaret McWhirter

I was sitting on Saturday 24th January 2021 waiting for word about whether my friend would be taken into hospital as she was positive with Covid-19. It was so bad here in Belfast that if you could possibly manage at home they thought it would be for the best. They had drafted in army medics to help out because the NHS was at breaking point.

She was taken into hospital that afternoon and put on fluids, antibiotics and oxygen in a Covid ward. She hadn't the breath to speak on the phone so all I could do was text her. Her daughter asked me to text as she was so glad to read them when she could. She hadn't the strength to text back but I sent one morning and night letting her know she was being thought of and who had been sending their good wishes. Then a big step forward I received a text from her on Sunday 31st January. The joy of knowing that my friend was on the mend was immense. She was still on nasal oxygen but was over the worse. Today Wednesday 3rd February I received a text to say she was getting home. I still can't go to see her as we are on lockdown until March 5th but the relief that she has been able to overcome this awful virus is overwhelming.

Margaret is 73 and originally from Suffolk. She has lived in Dundonald, Belfast for most of her adult life. Her son Michael's wedding has been put off twice. It was scheduled for July 2020, rescheduled for April 2021 and now the big date is September 2nd, 2021.

Café Society, 21st Century by Sally Willison

1964. Paris in midsummer. Along the Boulevard Ste Germaine cafés with people of many nationalities clustered around small tables, engaged in lively discourse, solving the world's problems. Red striped awnings bathed in a golden hue. Majestic plane trees lined the boulevard, looming solemn above the cacophony of *Deux Chevaux* and Peugeots. Man had not yet placed a foot on the moon. People read real books in real paper. They wrote letters in ink. Nevertheless, airplanes carried them to the destinations of their dreams. Nineteen years old and in love with love.

2021. Beaconsfield, Buckinghamshire in the spring. Along the Penn Road people from various ethnic and age groups gather outside or under cover at The Beech House. Lively discussion about the coronavirus and Brexit, peppered with lively gesticulations and, more often than not, shouts of rage. Laughter is scarce. Faces are stony. This is real. This is earnest. Even the stench of too many cars cannot drown out the smell of discontent. Man apparently placed a foot on the moon many moons before (but, strangely, not since). People now read books over their iPads. They send text messages and emails. Whoever writes a letter anymore? This is progress? Yet airplane travel to exotic places is no longer particularly desirable or an easy option. *Plus ça change.*

75 years old and longing for the past.

Choice by Tony McHale

When this is all over ... there will be partying 24/7, Pizza Hut will give away pizzas, Halley's comet will appear every hour on the hour, Christmas will happen five times a year, TV companies will ban all reality shows, Blackpool will become great again, fish'n'chips, burgers and chocolate will be healthy food, everyone will have great ideas when buying gifts for friends and relations, summers will be as we always remember them, stupid events will be taken out of the Olympics, everyone will see the Northern Lights, singing in the shower will be compulsory, vocation and aspiration will be reintroduced into the vernacular and the world will be totally integrated and at permanent peace ... or it'll just go back to what it was like before. Our choice.

Tony has written literally hundreds of hours of TV dramas from 'EastEnders' to 'Casualty', from 'The Bill' to 'Dalziel and Pascoe', from 'Silent Witness' to 'Waking the Dead'. He has created a number of original series such as 'Resort to Murder' and 'Headless', as well as co-creating 'Holby City' for which he received a BAFTA. Recently Tony has started writing novels. His first, 'Beck Le Street', is available on Amazon.

Nancy's Lockdown by Nancy Williams

I used to work in a nursery twice a week as a volunteer.

I also attended HiJinx Academy twice a week as well.

I went on regular holidays abroad and cruises.

I sang in a choir *Only Menopause Aloud* and we did lots of shows for charity.

I used to go to the pub for meals and have drinks.

I went shopping and played snooker sometimes or went bowling.

I enjoyed seeing people like my cousins and friends and seeing my papou and Uncle Ronnie in his care home.

I enjoyed staying with my Great Aunt Rene who will be 97 this year. I missed being with her for her birthday.

I loved going to the hairdresser and getting my nails done with my support worker who visited every Friday to take me out.

I looked forward to going to the theatre regularly to see musicals.

I went to London on a train to see friends.

I miss all of these things which were my life, very much.

I've started to learn the guitar in lockdown and enjoy singing Bob Marley's song 'Don't worry about a thing, 'cos every little thing is gonna be alright'.

Nancy is from Cardiff, South Wales and she has suffered from Dravet syndrome since she was six months old. Nancy appeared in Creative Ink's film, 'Dear John, Dear Anyone …'

Wearing Earrings in Lockdown by Liz Carew

Yesterday I wore my Sicilian earrings:
two turquoise globes with leaves and lemons;
I thought of terracotta houses and cobbled streets
winding up towards a gleaming Baroque church
dark and hushed inside, with a few tourists
gathered round a long-forgotten masterpiece.

The day before I wore my earrings from Valencia:
an outline of a stalk and single flower with four petals
that could be an infant's drawing or a Picasso sketch;
I dreamt of sampling spicy Tapas dishes
served in a shady courtyard with potted palms
and blue and white ceramic tiles.

Tomorrow I'll wear my Turkish earrings:
deep-red and orange tulip heads
with calligraphic flourishes round the edges;
I'll remember the view from our hotel room:
steep, huddled roofs, the outline of a mosque
a strip of Bosporus blue on the horizon.

The day after I'll wear my earrings from Bavaria:
hand-painted purple crocuses
on silver mounted wooden hearts;
I'll think of jagged peaks and Alpine pastures
churches with burnished onion domes
and pink and gold Rococo chapels

but today I'm wearing my Cotswold earrings:
tiny, pressed forget-me-nots under glass

just like the ones quietly invading
my flower beds and lawn
rooting me into the moment
and the glorious blooming of this fragile spring.

Liz comes from the north of Scotland, now lives in the Cotswolds and writes poetry and short stories.

The First Butterflies by Jane MacKinnon

Though 'normal' is a distant memory,
they'll be a time when we no longer live in fear.
Hope, at last, will grow stronger
And hope revives life's energy.

Along the hedgerows and woodland track,
brimstones declare that our winter has gone;
airborne primroses, they dance in the sun,
bright promises that 'normal' will come back.

For months beneath cold clods we lay;
now spring is not so far away.

Covid-Free Guernsey by Janet Rolfe

At last, Guernsey's second lockdown is over. I venture out in my rusty car, drive past real people with uncovered faces. Loading my supermarket trolley, I exchange smiles with a chap in the Free-From aisle. Strife-free, I chat with the check-out lady; pack shopping into the car and head for home.

Triumph is short-lived. There's a traffic jam – three school buses and a dozen angry cars. I divert down primrose lanes, reach the West Coast road. In celebration, we slightly exceed the speed limit of thirty-five miles an hour. The car is happy. I'm happy. Then we get whacked by a tsunami of Atlantic spray. Blinded, I flick all the levers and the wipers whizz over the windscreen. Sand and salt are swept away.

Serene, we trundle past cottages and solitary cyclists, to the place where a tower shouts at the sky. We saunter by the shut-down chippy at L'Eree Bay. No-one's by the sea, just mounds of vraic and the Guernsey breeze.

So, it's me, and the car singing Sarnia Cherie*, we're home at last, maskless and free.

*Sarnia Cherie – the anthem sung on Liberation Day, marking Guernsey's freedom after five wartime years of enemy rule.

Bunting by Charles Wickens

She's finished her home schooling, and now eight-year-old Molly sits with a pile of offcuts and a roll of binding tape in front of her. Tongue sticking out of the side of her mouth, she is cutting triangles from the material.

'What are you doing?' asks her mother.

'I'm making bunting,' she says, 'for when we get our people back.'

The summer wasn't too bad – no physical contact, but at least you could sit in the garden together, some sort of normality in the sun. You could talk about The Blitz spirit and say it could be worse and at least we haven't caught it yet.

Then winter. Upper lips unstiffening, stir-craziness setting in. Bugger The Blitz! – people are dying, and you can't hug your granny through a fuzzy screen that pixilates and pauses.

But now, as Molly wields her pinking shears, there is expectation in the air, for now we have a road map, and now we have embarked on a journey towards the longest, and, we hope, most joyful day.

We shall hold the party to end all parties, and Molly's bunting will be proudly hung all through the house.

When we get our people back.

Charles has published four books on Amazon Kindle. 'The Diary of an Unfortunate Man'. 'Go-Down-To-Come-Up' is a science fiction adventure for older children. 'What I Done in The Blitz' is the story of a young man's sexual awakening in World War Two and 'Jones & Me', a set of short stories about childhood in 1950s' south London. His latest book 'The Sir Acton Turville Company of Peripatetic Thespians' is a theatrical yarn set in the early 1800s.

Morning Always Comes by Keith Chatfield

The threads of fear are interwoven in
my every thought, but I am not alone.

The weight of tiredness, even after sleep,
impairs my mind, but I am not alone.

The suff'ring that engulfs our world disrupts
my way of life, but I am not alone.

For I am one of multi-millions who
reach back for multi-centuries and this,
I see so clearly now, is all just part
of life. I cannot run from it, but need
to hang awhile in solidarity
with all humanity. This somehow makes
us one, and any healing that I crave
is bound with others' healing. So we need
to glean the clues from out this season of
disruption to transport us to a world
far better than the one we knew and loved.

Curtailing of ability to work
and play and live and breathe at will may all
be new to me but is normality
for so, so many millions. I am now
reminded of their plight. Such shattered lives
cannot be healed by individuals.

The morning must not light my life without
it lighting that of others. I need them

and they need me to make a change so that,
when morning comes, as come it will, we all
may share its light.

*Keith wrote and narrated children's stories for ITV:
'HattyTown' and 'Issi Noho'. Books include: 'HattyTown Tales',
'Issi Noho', 'Issi Pandemonium', 'Issi's Magic Tonic', 'Issi's
Magic Ups & Downs', 'Tregarrick Adventure', 'Bird Mountain',
'My Brother Humphrey'. Play: 'Riot Monday' 2013. Established
QWriters: workshops for those interested in writing for Quakers
and friends of Quakers.*

When This Damned Thing Is Over ... by Hilary Bates

I will hug you and kiss you and ruffle your hair,
dance with you, laugh with you, live moments to share,
sit with you, comfort you, tell you I care.
Start a new life with you. This is my prayer.

Riding Bikes and Giving Vaccines by Babs Young
Health Care Professional, Immunisation

Who would have thought it? Out of retirement and working at the age of 67!

I answered the request for retired nurses to support the NHS at the beginning of the Covid pandemic last year. My skills were not needed then, but in December the call came out for nurses to join the mass vaccination programme. An opportunity not to be missed: that feeling of contributing to something never achieved before and also, very personally, to relieve the daily tedium of being at home with no focus. I hadn't actually given an injection for over twenty years, but surely it's like riding a bike? So they say.

Numerous online training modules and an extensive application and vetting process later and I am now a Health Care Professional, Immunisation, working for the flexi bank for the local NHS Community Trust. I've worked in a disused Debenhams store in Folkestone and a state-of-the-art empty call centre in Ramsgate. I'm meeting new colleagues and others who I worked with years ago. All working extra hours to achieve our national goal. I'm in awe of the volunteers who also give their time so freely. The atmosphere is one of professionalism, purpose and fun. The staff are happy to be there and the patients are so grateful. Many come in with trepidation and are anxious but they almost skip out wearing their bravery sticker and carrying their vaccination card.

I aim to continue for as long as I am needed. This has shown me that we are never too old to play our part in whatever way we can. ... and yes, giving an injection is like riding a bike! Apparently I have an excellent technique.

Babs trained as a nurse at Westminster Hospital and worked in the NHS as a nurse, health visitor and in Nurse Education until she retired.

Blood Brothers by Peter Keeble

Mark this thin syringe slide through my skin.
The undead virus from the phial
mingles with my blood.
Though I may wince and cringe
it martials unknowing denizens
deep within.

And soon a million,
and millions more and we will no more
stand and shiver a coffin's length apart
or shout and strain to hear,
but find again the trust
to hold a hand and heal a heart.

Peter lives in Harrow, London. He is a former participant in Metroland Poets and author of 'Passengers and Other Poems' available on www.pwkeeble.wixsite.com/poetryetc or from his publisher, Demsey & Windle: www.dempseyandwindle.com/peter-keeble.html

Walking in Hope by Jill Wallis

When you were sick I took you walking
in soft spring sunshine, along the cool canal.
We had no hope, just love, trust and each other.
But then you left.

And afterwards I took my grief out walking
back along familiar towpaths
in sunshine, wind and drenching rain.
Grief did not leave me sadly
but perhaps the worst of it,
the bitter, clotted rags and shreds,
did peel away and melt into the wind.

But now the world is sick.
Too much for me to carry by myself
and the rule is – all must walk alone.
So this time I'm taking Hope out walking by my side
under lark-song, by green water, cold and clear.

Hope for myself, my family, my community
that all will once again be well,
that no-one else will leave
and we will walk again together in the sun.

Hope too that in each far community, each family,
someone like me is walking out
on streets, in fields, by rivers, parks, in tightly packed and
seething slums,
just walking
with Hope.

Jill has published her prize-winning anthology 'Dialogue for One'/ The Littoral Press. She is a retired lecturer who published her anthology following the premature death of her husband and is currently studying for a doctorate to keep her brain cells active. She was Editor of 'Rhyme & Reason' from 2010 until its demise in 2018.

Living On by Shirley Rose

I am in a bubble with my younger son Daren who orders books for me on Amazon. I lost my husband Derek in 2007 and my eldest son Stuart the following year in 2008. Stuart took so long in coming and always dressed so dapper. I go for long socially distanced walks with my friend and she says, 'You always talk about Derek and Stuart as though they are here'.

For me they are and I like to talk about the fun times. On the family grave are the words: *To live in the hearts of those we love is to never to die.* Thomas Campbell (1777-1844)

Shirley is from the East End of London.

2020-2021 Diary by Jennifer Dannhauser

February 2020: the world was normal. I went on holiday.

March 2020: the cracks started to show. I was prosecuting a kidnap case. One juror failed to show. Then another. Defence counsel and I held our breath, trying to eek this case to its conclusion before we fell below the required nine jurors. We did it. A sentence of four years imprisonment. Little did I know, we were about to enter a sentence all of our own. My husband told me to buy toilet roll, canned goods and facemasks. I laughed. Then nurseries closed. This was no laughing matter. I was heavily pregnant and on full time kiddy-care with a three-year-old come teenager. I longed for the days when Brexit was the big problem.

April 2020: your baby is upside down and too small. We need to get her out early. *My* world was upside down and very small. I was alone for all but the very end of the two-day process. But she was perfect.

Summer 2020: is the world getting back to normal? We booked holidays for early 2021. But then … second lockdown, Christmas cancelled, school cancelled. But Early Years Childcare can remain open. Yes, Boris. Squeals of delight from post-September 2016 parents.

February 2021: we should have been on holiday. Instead, the lockdown baby went to nursery. It blew her mind.

March 2021: back to work, mostly via a computer screen. But when I did go to court – Perspex screens everywhere. Although my client still simply used his mask as a chin hammock.

21st June 2021: the world was normal? Holiday? TBC …

Jennifer is a criminal barrister, mother of two and wine connoisseur although not necessarily in that order. She has performed in three Creative Ink plays and the film, 'Dear John, Dear Anyone …'

In a State by Louise Norton

Get up, get down
same chair, same mind
get in, get out,
same bed, same side.
Never knew my walls so well.
Today is the first anniversary
of Lockdown Hell.
23rd March 2021

A Tale of Two Seasons by Jamie Dannhauser

'It was the best of times, it was the worst of times.' So wrote Dickens. But even more apt are the words that follow: 'it was the age of wisdom, it was the age of foolishness … it was the spring of hope, it was the winter of despair'.

How contagious Britain mirrors revolting France…

Spring 2020: the sky was clear, the sun was shining, no more commuting meant precious time with my wife Jen and daughter Maddie – and then, little Ellie came peacefully into the world (as she has been ever since); coronavirus fear gripped the country but the worst was behind us; Boris told us it would soon be over, Maddie could get back to the trampoline park.

Winter 2020: the days were grim, schools were shutting and mutant variants stalked all of us; the NHS was crippled and the Christmas 'it would be inhuman to cancel', was cancelled; that nursery stayed open was a godsend – at least Maddie could enjoy some semblance of life as it should be.

Spring 2021: 110,000 excess deaths, borders closed but mass vaccination tantalizingly dangling the prospect of normality (and the trampoline park) in front of us all.

A year on, tragically, wisdom is still in short supply, foolishness abounds. But then what has changed?

The 'season of light' cannot arrive quickly enough.

Jamie is an economist by day and adoring dad/husband the rest of the time. Saddened by events of the last year. Hopeful that we never again sacrifice society's future to preserve a part of its present. He brought light to Creative Ink plays and appeared in their film, 'Dear John, Dear Anyone …'

Relief by Doctor Ryan Cholwill

What will it be like
to see the children smile again
instead of trying to read their eyes?

What will it be like
to work without barriers between us
instead of trying to make spaces between our words six feet
wide?

What will it be like
to know my patients are not harbouring the enemy
instead of squinting at them with a suspicious mind?

It will be like taking off that claustrophobic mask
at the end of the long exhausting day
and breathing the crisp cold evening air …

Ryan is a GP in Cape Town, South Africa.

At the Light Behind and Within by Steve Givens

Life, or some microscopic viral version of it,
jostled us into closer proximity with ourselves and a few
others
hunkered down and holed up
somewhere deep.

Like neighbor farmers waving across fields and fences
we walked separate but parallel lives
hoeing our own rows,
planting seeds we could never imagine
would grow in such seclusion.
But so much life happens down in the rich darkness
we cannot see.

We sprouted anew,
delicate, fragile things
waiting for wind to blow,
discovered how we might bend,
find resilience and strength
in gifts of faith, hope and love
we had already been given.

In the end, we learned,
sometimes the very best we can do
is grow where we are planted,
come to rest
let the light behind and within
shine through.

A 'Rhyme & Reason' editor in 1996, Steve lived, wrote and taught in Buckinghamshire for a few years in the 1990s, before moving back home to America's Midwest, St Louis, Missouri, USA.

Solace by Rosie Moore

Whose are the hands that cast stars into space?
Who holds the oceans in a bowl?
Who births each day
and all it contains –
who has that control?
My Covid-fuddled brain is not
so weak that I can't recognize
the power of my dynamic God,
and one great truth I realize:
He holds us in those hands.

Rosie is from Belfast (60 something, still thinks she's 16).

Home by Debbie Bennell
Clinical Nurse Specialist
at the Rennie Grove Hospice Care

I feel deeply for my Critical Care nursing colleagues and have felt guilty for not being there alongside them. For the last few years I have worked in the community. Life has changed but I have laughed whilst trying to put on PPE in the howling winds, whilst waiting for my glasses to demist so that I can see who I am talking to. I have felt like crying just wanting to give a hug to let them know I am there for them. I see families together, because they now have time and have chosen to care for their loved ones at home. It has been a privilege to walk alongside our patients and families and share the last chapter, guiding, supporting, to ensure that each patient has the chance to live their best life to the last day.

Time is very precious and for years we have just run out of it. Now we have had the opportunity to reset. Saying a final farewell is special, particularly when a loved one peacefully dies in their own familiar surroundings with the people that matter the most.

The sun is shining, the birds are singing, nature is bursting through and there is real hope for the future.

Debbie worked as a sister in Critical Care for eleven years and transitioned to Palliative Care in the community where she has worked for the last twelve years and her most recent challenge was to become a Queen's Nurse. She writes that few other professions allow you to meet so many people from all walks of life and know that you can actually make a difference to their journey through life.

Care by David A Paton

When you care
you don't despair.
You feel everyone
with you there.

As you partake
of your role,
you feel ennobled
as a whole.

Bringing joy to a
person's life,
you light the way
with peace and delight.

Making many wonderful memories
full of love, hugs and sparkle.
We cherish these
under our favourite tree.

*David is from Dundee in Scotland. He writes that his
wonderful mother, Margaret, passed away in Cupar on 12th May
2020. She had dementia and became a victim of Covid-19. Having
worked in a delightful care home for the elderly in Chalfont St
Peter, South Buckinghamshire, David now continues to look after
older people in a care home in Dundee.*

***Fear, Exhaustion, Strength** by Samantha Howard*
Director of Nursing and Patient Services
at the Rennie Grove Hospice Care

When I started in my post as Director of Nursing for the Rennie Grove Hospice in May 2019, I could never have envisaged, even in my wildest dreams, what the first eighteen months would hold. What a roller coaster ride – up and down, round the corners and even upside down at times. There were some points where it felt there was no safety harness and I was just holding on as tight as I could.

Fear was the biggest emotion we had to deal with: fear for the nurses who were scared of contracting this virus and taking it home to their families, bringing it back into the office or even worse, giving it to our fragile, vulnerable patients. Fear for our patients who knew they were dying and were desperately trying to live their last days and weeks at home where they wanted to be surrounded by their families, who were many times told they couldn't visit.

The guidance on what we should be doing changed on an almost daily basis which added to the fear and caused doubt in what we were doing and then we couldn't get the masks, gloves and aprons we needed as we weren't the NHS.

One year on and we survived! We worked as one, we supported each other, our confidence grew and we have emerged stronger than ever but we are exhausted.

Samantha grew up in South Cheshire and moved to London at eighteen to do her nurse training. She lived in Watford, Hertfordshire for 30 years before moving to Leighton Buzzard, Bedfordshire during the pandemic.

What Has Been Happening by Charlotte Develin
Intensive Care Matron at Guy's and St Thomas's
NHS Foundation Trust, London.

During the pandemic we peaked at over 200 ICU patients; this was a phenomenal team effort from everyone involved but the pain, exhaustion and heartbreak that went into this has been immeasurable. It has changed me as a person; it has changed the staff I manage and the NHS will never be the same again.

When this is over I won't have to feel guilt. Guilt that I couldn't stop the patients getting sick and dying. Guilt for the families robbed of time at their loved ones' bedside. Guilt that the staff who I am supposed to protect are in painful PPE for hours on end with staffing ratios we would never have dreamed of. Guilt for the staff who have been pulled from the wards to help, terrified. Guilt that this experience has been so all-consuming that I have pushed those close to me away because I don't have the words to explain.

When this is over the stresses, the frustrations, my job defining me as a person will disappear into memories, like a bad dream. Then I will take back my life and move on ...

Charlotte went to the University of West of England to study for her degree in nursing and has nursed in Bristol and the intensive care unit at St Mary's, Paddington where she also studied for her Intensive Care qualification. She worked for four years in the intensive care unit at the new Fiona Stanley Hospital, Perth, Australia. She came back to London in 2018 working initially as ICU matron at King's College Hospital and for the last two years as ICU matron at Guy's and Thomas's Hospital. Charlotte lives in Putney, south-west London.

A Life in the Day of … Doctor Amy from Brighton

It's no stranger to us, we've dealt with it a thousand times
before.

Finger to carotid, stethoscope to chest, no life. Sign the
certificate.

Bring in the families, sit them down and tell them the worst
in unambiguous terms.

I'd call myself a sensitive and seasoned pro when it comes to
it.

It rarely goes home with me. There's been the odd case, but
mostly to me, it's just my job.

Compartmentalization. A concept I learned from an army
colonel. A mate's dad.

'On the phone, bullets flying, but voice steady not to scare the
wife.'

I carried that through my training and early career.

But the neat little boxes of my life wouldn't close shut now.

This is 2020, and there's a new normal.

Hadn't normalized this yet.

Frail old man, no hope with this thing. Nothing more I can
offer.

The decision to palliate, the logical way forward. Vacant
written on his face.

Written in the notes. *Check.*

Check him once more before I go.

Can I help with pain? Any terminal agitation?

Chest still, no life. Sign the certificate.

I ask the nurse, 'Who's next of kin?' The wife they say.
Oh and by the way, she's downstairs, just come through A&E.
I go to check. No one's told her where her husband went
or with what she should be admitted.
Which comes first? I break both to her. Total shock.
Literal silence at a best friend lost.
She wants to go upstairs and touch the hand that had always
held hers so tight.

Wheeled her then back. Brevity because the influx means
we need the beds for the wave that doesn't ebb even at three
am.
As if it weren't bad enough, panic strikes when I realize she's
pulled the ticket, with her PCR
to be the next customer for that bed slot.
Unknowingly in the queue for that death spot.
Nurses' station alive shuffling a few around so this poor
woman isn't sentenced in the same room where she'd said
goodbye to that much loved man.

Throughout the pandemic, this was the only family member
Amy informed of a death in person. She writes: 'I know that rules
to keep others safe necessitated barriers when coming into hospital
to visit. But I am so sorry for every family that received bad news,
had to say goodbye over FaceTime or were woken in the middle of
the night with sad news sooner than expected, without having a
chance to comfort and hold their loved ones in their last days and
hours. The grief expressed by families has been so different because
of this, and that's been heartbreaking to watch'.

Hope by Gill Hartley

Like me, the garden is desolate,
the mantle of winter has cast us both down.
Seed heads have replaced the flowers,
the rose arch is a bower of thorns.
The hammock where we swung on sunlit evenings,
stands dormant in the dank, anaemic air.
Everything looks abandoned,
bleak and starved of light.
The garden, like me, is bereaved,
now summer has turned into night.

This morning, I searched the sleeping garden,
trod the sodden, yellowed grass,
knelt amongst the hibernating bushes,
cast aside the crumbling leaves,

and then I found
a thrusting shoot of crocus.

Gill's poetry collection 'My True Son' and 'Aspects of Loss', an anthology she edited and published by Moorleys, followed the unexpected loss of her 22-year-old son Will. All profits go to Compassionate Friends, a charity supporting bereaved parents and their families. Gill was Editor of 'Rhyme & Reason' in 1993 and 1994.

A-levels, Alpha variant, Amazon deliveries, antibodies, antidote, antiseptic wipes, apps, asymptomatic, Baking banana bread, BAME, Barnard Castle, bats, bin day, birdwatching, Black Lives, booster, Boris Johnson, Brazilian strain, briefings, bubble, bumpy, Captain Sir Tom Moore, care homes, casualties, China, Clap for Carers, cleaning cupboards, coffee, continuous cough, coronavirus, Covid-19, crisis, curve, cyclists, Daily figures, data, death toll, decontamination, Delta variant, dexamethasone, disinfectant, DIY, Doctor Anthony Fauci, Dolly Parton, Dominic Cummings, Donald Trump, dose, Eat Out to Help Out, efficacy, efficiency, elbow bumps, exponential, E484k, Fake news, fines, food deliveries, fundraising, Gardens, GCSEs, germs, GPs, graphs, green list, Hair, hand cream, herd immunity, heroes, holiday refunds, home, home improvements, home schooling, hope, hospitals, ICU, immune system, immunization, Indian variant, infections, influencers, inoculation, isolation, Jabs, jig-saw puzzles, Joe Wicks, joggers, Keep fit, Kent strain, key workers, Kleenex, Local heroes, lockdown, long Covid, loved ones, Masks, Matt Hancock, memes, mental health, misinformation, Moderna, mutation, New normal, NHS, Nightingale Hospitals, Novavax, Online deliveries, online support, outdoors, Oxford-AstraZeneca, Pandemic, pangolin, panic buying, passports, peaks, Pfizer, phases, picnics, plastic gloves, PPE, Professor Chris Whitty, Professor Van-Tam, Quarantine, Rainbows, R Factor, recession, red list, remote consultations, respirator, restrictions, road map, Rona, rule of six, Scrabble, shielding, slides, social distancing, South African strain, space, spike, stay at home, staycation, stay safe, stockpiling, support bubbles, swab, Takeaways, test and trace, tiers, toilet rolls, toothache, traffic light system, transmission, travel corridors, travel insurance, two metres apart, Underlying health conditions, unprecedented, Vaccinators, vaccine, vaccine certificates, vaccine passports, variant, ventilation, ventilators, victims, virtual, virus, visors, vitamin D, volunteers, vulnerable, Walking, wash hands, waves, weddings, WFH, WHO, wine deliveries, woolly hats, Wuhan, Xmas, Years 2020-2021, Zero transmissions, Zoom.

The Final Word … is all yours. These pages have been left blank for you to document your own pandemic story, in whatever form you think fit. Keep this, your own time capsule, somewhere safe.

Printed in Great Britain
by Amazon